THEORY NOW

Other Theory Writings by the Author

Filmspeak and *Why Theory?*

Theory Now

Films, Television, and Ralph Cohen's Method

EDWARD L. TOMARKEN

ALPERT BOOKS

British Library Cataloguing in Publication Data
A catalogue record for this book is available from the British Library

ISBN 978-1-8381859-0-9

Typeset by Amolibros, Milverton, Somerset
This book production has been managed by Amolibros
www.amolibros.com
Printed and bound by Lightning Source

Dedication

In Memory of my Parents, Barney and Pearl Tomarken

List of Visual Materials

CHAPTER ONE

David Cronenberg's *eXistenZ*, 1999
Phoebe Waller-Bridge's *Fleabag*, 2018
Neil Gaiman's *Good Omens*, Episode 1, 2019
Nancy Meyers' *The Parent Trap*, 1990

CHAPTER TWO

Eric Kripke's *The Boys*, episode 6, 2019
Sharon Maguire's *Bridget Jones's Baby*, 2017
Robert Doherty's *Elementary*, season 5, episode 2, 2016

CHAPTER THREE

Neil Gaiman's *Good Omens*, episode 3, 2019
Jon S. Baird's *Stan and Ollie*, 2018
Henning Mankell's *Wallander*, series 4, episode 6, 2010

CHAPTER FOUR

Peter Farrelly's *Green Book*, 2018
Robert Quinn's *The Bay*, episode 6, 2019
Jerry Bruckheimer's *Lucifer*, episode 3, 2017

CHAPTER FIVE

CHAPTER SIX

Table of Contents

Acknowledgements

Evander Lomke was the first person to encourage me in this project, editing, publishing *Filmspeak* and providing valuable suggestions for the other two volumes. Many people too numerous to name have given me valuable advice about films and television programmes, particularly, Emma, Beau, and Jamie Grimes. Two who deserve special mention pointed to programmes used in the text, Gillian Powell for *Elementary* and Peter Hansen for *The Boys*. Amy Myers has generously offered expert advice in this new venture for me of self-publishing. Dr. Ana Maria Sousa Aguiar de Medeiros made helpful recommendations about publishers. Lenham Square designed the cover with careful attention to the content of the book and within a strict deadline. My thanks to Jane Tatam of Amolibros for page design and proofreading the book. My greatest debt, as ever, is to my wife, who guided me and the book through its various stages, from encouraging clarification of my ideas to meticulous proofreading.

Introduction

My two previous volumes on literary theory focused upon the period of the 1960s and 70s, from Foucault to Cixous (*Filmspeak*, 2012), and then moved to the 1980s and 90s, ranging from Geertz to Nussbaum (*Why Theory?*, 2017). Covering the period from 2000 to the present, this work will focus on essays by less well-known critics who have not yet achieved the status of those in the previous volumes. My choice of selections represents an important change in the nature of theory since 2000. Instead of relying on the great names of theory from the twentieth century, present-day theory is dominated by essays that focus upon specific literary and literary-historical problems and do not attempt to formulate complete or all-encompassing theories.

This new era of eclecticism helps explain why many twenty-first century theorists, in addition to combining older theories, focus on specific works of art and limited moments in literary history. The implication is that these essays on local and specific theoretical problems, the tesserae, will eventually fit into the larger mosaic of literary theory as a whole, but that new larger frameworks will develop slowly, resulting from group endeavours, and be different in kind from previous theories. In my view, this movement of the last twenty years suggests that literary theory is coming into its own, asserting that its very structure will be different from theories of the past.

Concomitant with this specific, eclectic approach and bound up with it, is the rise of genre theory, a kind of theory that is broader and more accommodating than most positions of the last century. Although widespread and prevalent, genre theory is difficult to define and describe, in part because it is open to so many kinds of approaches and because most practitioners devote themselves to concrete problems, not to an overall theory. However, the appearance of John Rowlett's edition of *Ralph Cohen's Genre Theory and Historical Change* represents a turning point. This collection of essays presents the first formulation of a comprehensive genre theory. As Rowlett points out in his introduction, the raw materials are now available to complete this task:

> While Cohen's literary experiments have been salutary to his students and his other readers during a time of rapid and often incomprehensible change, they deserve a much wider audience since Cohen himself is the scholar whose theoretical work on genre, I suggest, exceeds competing procedures, such as those more narrowly focused on lyrical poetry, novel theory, narrative theory, or cultural theory. That is because, for dealing with the implications of such historical change, his is the most precise, systematic, effective, and inclusive. It is also the most comprehensive, since in proposing a genre theory suited to describing and analyzing generic change, Cohen makes possible an exploration of the functions of change in the making of society. And to whom is that alien (Rowlett, xiii)?

The present volume is devoted to demonstrating the precision, effectiveness, systematic inclusiveness and comprehensiveness of Ralph Cohen's theory of genre. The need for such a book is exemplified by Rowlett's work, which is comprised of twenty essays on various subjects, eight of which had not before been published. The range of topics and the variety of subject matter present a challenge to the search for consistent principles. But at the same time, the sheer variety and range of penetrating analysis contained in the essays speaks to the present state of theory: critics are more interested in theoretically informed considerations of concrete literary and literary historical problems than in totalising systems. But here I confront a massive problem; how to present a systematic and comprehensive account of Cohen's genre theory without resorting to a totalizing system?

The first and most important point to make about Cohen's theory of genre is that it is historical and governed by the changes in history that none of us can predict or wholly anticipate. In that very important sense no historical theory of genre can be totalizing; we are all in James Joyce's nightmare of history and that includes our theories of genre: it is, however, comprehensive in that I know of no aesthetic theory—aside from a marginal scientific or mathematical concept that would replace or eliminate the aesthetic—that cannot be accommodated by Cohen's genre theory. Nonetheless, defining genre theory is a complex matter: my aim is to describe some of the rudimentary elements toward that process. Cohen often pointed out to us in class that many of the most difficult ideas can only be understood in negative terms, that is, by way of what they are not, so I propose to begin by describing what genre theory is not. Ideology does not inhere, he asserted, in any genre. Ideology was and is a function of how the writer and reader use genre, not of genre itself. I begin with this negative principle to suggest Cohen's genre theory is accommodating to most theories but not to all and that my manner of proceeding will be less to build a Leviathan of genre than to articulate some principles that will be open to most, but not all kinds of theories.

First, a few words about the history of genre theory. This topic is itself worthy of a book and my goal here is only to suggest very briefly how Cohen built upon the work of his predecessors. Alastair Fowler, his colleague at the University of Virginia, provided probably the most erudite and comprehensive history of genre criticism, demonstrating how an understanding of the history of a genre enriches our interpretation of any work of literature. In agreement with Bakhtin, Cohen accepts that genres derive from general language usage, both oral and written, and that historical changes of style involve an interrelationship between genre and language in everyday communication. Like Yury Tynyanov, Cohen argues that genres are dynamic systems involving hierarchies that change throughout history and that new genres are made up of old genres, both notions reinforced by the work of Rosalie Colie. Like Gérard Genette, Cohen distinguishes modes from genres on the grounds that genres are historical in nature while modes are what Northrop Frye calls "radicals of presentation", that is, rhetorical devices chosen by the writer. While sharing with Frye the rhetorical element of genre, Cohen believes that Frye's focus on modes leaves out of consideration the historical element of genres. In opposition to Derrida, Cohen argues that genres do not have laws but are marked by what Wittgenstein called "family resemblance": all genres are subject to change, both minor and major, and their evolution may result in periods in which they are neglected or may even disappear. Finally, Cohen accepts Fredric Jameson's contractual concept of genre but, as mentioned earlier, does not believe that economic concepts or ideologies inhere in genres. However, Cohen's theory moves beyond that of any of his predecessors in that it points to aesthetic interpretation as a form of knowledge no different from knowledge in any other field, a topic pursued in Chapter Six and the Conclusion.

My approach in this study is to follow Cohen's example and avoid any attempt to define the essence of genre theory. Instead, I shall describe six principles or axioms that will be of use not only in analysis of the arts but toward a theory of knowledge in general. As already mentioned, the application of genre to learning will be discussed in more detail in the final chapter and the conclusion.

At this point I wish to emphasise that as a theory of learning, not limited to literary theory, Cohen's concept of genre goes beyond that of his predecessors. One example may suggest the direction of my argument. A recent newspaper article discussed a procedure that permitted new and clearer distinctions between different types of breast cancer, further refining individual physical responses to the disease and to the various therapies. This discovery would serve to improve treatment by combining consideration of the kind of breast cancer in relation to the type of procedure. In a sense, it becomes a form of generic interpretation, an understanding of the various aspects of a genre in conjunction with a consideration of which generic elements would be most fruitful and appropriate.

The bridge here between the type of cancer and the patient, the genre and the work of art, is the term 'interpretation'. Have we now reached the stage of medical history when we realise that major decisions about health involve not only science and technology but also interpretation? With an increasingly older population, doctors face patients with multiple life-threatening conditions and must also keep in mind how treatment(s) impact on quality of life. Of course, the choice is usually left to the patient, but an informed decision is dependent upon the advice of the physician, advice that must go well beyond the technical elements of therapy. Interpretation cannot be avoided. If interpretation is a procedure shared by the sciences and the humanities, then genre theory applies to all forms of knowledge. My final chapter and conclusion will explain why interpretation is increasingly necessary.

My interest in the general relevance of genre theory as a form of knowledge is one of the main reasons for continuing with the procedure used in my first two volumes on literary theory, which used films and television to illustrate genre theory. The visual examples help demonstrate that the concepts apply well beyond literature and the arts and that the ideas involved are not merely academic and erudite but also available in popular culture. As pointed out in the two previous volumes, I make no claim to any expertise in the visual arts; my analysis may seem unsophisticated to specialists in film, television and other visual media. However, the purpose of this project is not to offer innovative views of the visual materials but to provide clarification of the genre concepts. Like the physician in the previous example, my object in presenting somewhat technical aspects of genre theory in a form available to a general audience—in popular films and television programmes—is to demonstrate how these principles are involved in our everyday life and can be understood by those who are not experts in the field.

The book is divided into six chapters, each focusing upon a principle or axiom that will provide, I believe, the framework for a systematic and comprehensive theory of genre. Each chapter consists of three sections (except for Chapter One that has four), made up of an essay and a visual example, a film or a television programme. Most of the essays appeared in *New Literary History* under Ralph Cohen's editorship: one essay in each chapter is from another journal to demonstrate that the issues considered were of broad concern in the field. But Cohen as an editor was unique in that he often gathered the best in the field and brought out the best in the best. Moreover, the arrangement of the essays in the various volumes amounted to a form of ventriloquism, the individual essays arranged so that together they interacted to suggest something beyond their own positions, somehow speaking for Cohen.

In my study of Samuel Johnson's edition of Shakespeare, I discovered Johnson's variorum technique—the Variorum edition of Shakespeare prints at the bottom of each page a collection of critical remarks on a passage or word with some pages comprised of one word of the play and the rest commentary in small print. Johnson is selective in his choice of commentary, his aim being to show that in relation to one another the critics impart a different position than their own, one more like that of Johnson. Cohen introduced me to Johnson in a senior undergraduate seminar. As

I worked on the present project a Johnsonian strategy appeared in volumes of *New Literary History* edited by Cohen. My own imitation of this strategy is to juxtapose *NLH* essays with those of other journals, not only to show that interest in genre is widespread in the field but also that the interchange between articles suggests new ideas about genre not found in any of the essays on their own. Often, these interactive ideas are manifested and clarified by the visual materials.

The first chapter, "Gooey Genre: Escape from Rules and Laws", is designed to show that Cohen's concept of genre is a flexible one that permits change both revolutionary and evolutionary. Furthermore, each new example of a genre alters not only the genre itself but also the system of genres: this hierarchy is subject to change and is affected, whether subtly or overtly, by every single work of its kind. In short, the classical concept of genres as fixed categories or pigeonholes is gone: the restrictions of genre cannot be essentialized into rules or laws. The most prominent evidence for the passing out of history of a concept of genre as governed by rules and laws is the fact that almost all artists combine genres— including classical writers, as we shall see in Chapter Three— making it impossible to follow any rules or laws that clearly vary from one genre to another.

Because of the prevalence of genres in combination, Chapter Two considers Cohen's view that study of genre combinations is often a key to interpretation. Once we put aside the old notion of genres as rules applied from above or apart from the intent of the artist/writer, we can see that the genres chosen by the writer, like the material selected by the visual artist, bear directly upon individual artistic goals. And aesthetic aims are a useful place to begin the process of interpretation. But interpretation, like genres and genre hierarchies, is subject to historical change. For instance, we do not in the present day respond to the epic in the way that people did in the time of John Milton. In using the epic as well as other genres in *Paradise Lost*, Milton was placing his poem at the top of the genre hierarchy of his era, and yet little more than a century later Samuel Johnson, with less reverence for the genre, remarked of the great epic that "none ever wished it longer".

The changes of history involve genres and responses to or interpretations of genre. Chapter Three considers this problem. In particular, our understanding of the aims and purposes of genres and artistic generic choices involves a new kind of literary history. History is seen, using a metaphor of Hans Robert Jauss, as similar to a planetary system like our own solar system. The various disciplines—from literary theory and sociology to biology and physics—are planets with their own orbits, yet subject to the larger orbit of the galaxy of the solar system or history. New literary history serves to show that literary history has an orbit, its own history, that is different from that of other disciplinary orbits while joining with all others in being ultimately subsumed in the all-encompassing system of history. Crossing from one discipline to another thus involves entering into a different orbit, the subject of the next chapter.

Chapter Four considers how genres change with disciplines and that crossing from one discipline to another may enrich or throw into question the approach accepted within a discipline. Most philosophers, for example, assume that Socrates speaks for Plato, but as a literary critic, Dorrit Cohn, points out, Plato used the genre of the dialogue and permitted Socrates to argue for views directly opposed to Plato's own practice. Ralph Cohen argues that moving between disciplines helps resolve intractable problems within a field and also results in new sorts of relationships being formed between different disciplines. Could Plato be suggesting some modification of Socrates' philosophy and can the Platonic dialogue be seen as both literary and philosophical? The interrelations of disciplines highlight how knowledge is subject to change, not only due to the historical circumstances beyond the control of learners—-events taking place outside the walls of schools and universities—but also from within when a biologist crosses the hall to enter a literary seminar or a sculptor looks into the microscope. And genre, which is both ever changing and unchanging, a still point of the turning wheel—to use a favourite metaphor of Northrop Frye—is a means of studying change, the topic of the next chapter.

Chapter Five considers the study of change, since, as Cohen argues, change is central to all knowledge: subject to the flow of time, we can only identify any object or event in the flux or continuous flow of history by way of difference or change. The point about change is that by its very nature it involves an alteration from something else, so change must involve constancy, an alternative to what has changed. A genre meets precisely that paradoxical need, changing with every use or application but still recognisable as a genre and, in that respect, unchanged. Cohen proposes that change should be approached by way of the distinction between innovation and variation, radical change as opposed to incremental development. He argues that analysis of change involves an understanding of what he calls social norms, basic premises that are taken for granted in a historical period. For instance, Pope in *The Rape of the Lock* tells us that Belinda "On her white Breast a sparkling Cross she wore, / Which Jews might kiss, and Infidels adore." (Canto II, 8-9). The question for the literary historian is what change is suggested by this ornamental form of religion: religious practice and the social decorum of its symbols or the eccentric use that people like Belinda make of such symbols. Has the nature of Christian symbols changed or is Belinda exploiting a religious object to call attention to her cleavage? We can begin to see how interpretation of change, in this instance literary interpretation, involves a good deal more than disciplinary-specific knowledge. Something more is required for understanding genres, something like knowledge of the world, the topic of Chapter Six.

In this final chapter, I venture into an area that Cohen often pointed toward but did not himself characterise in detail. One of his favourite quotations in this regard was Samuel Johnson's remark that "life must be seen before it can be known". The chapter pursues a suggestion from John Rowlett's introduction that Cohen's genre theory is rhizomatic. The reference here is to Deleuze and Guattari's distinction between two kinds of development or growth, that of tree roots as opposed to that of the rhizome. The former grows only in a linear or up and down direction, but the latter, in addition to vertical movement, is capable of lateral growth. Cohen implies that genres develop like rhizomes and that the rate and direction of development may vary. While Cohen argues that the historical changes of genre are related to culture or social history, I suggest the reverse is also possible, that literary development may reveal something about the culture, in Marianne Moore's terms, "imaginary gardens with real toads" (*Poetry*, 1919). In this way, I attempt to show how genre analysis of the arts relates to life and is a form of knowledge, keeping in mind, as Cohen asserts repeatedly, that literary knowledge is not different in kind from any other kind of knowledge.

My conclusion consists of an analysis of one of the earliest of Cohen's publications, first published in 1965. In an edition of *Huckleberry Finn*, Cohen added an appendix of "Special Aids". Here I find all the seeds of the full-grown flowers that became his theory of genre. And, most importantly, the relation of genre analysis to life is more prominent here than in any of his other writings.

Chapter One

Gooey Genre: Escape from Laws and Rules

I Teresa de Lauretis, "Becoming Inorganic", *Critical Inquiry*, 29, 4, 2003 and David Cronenberg's *eXistenZ*, 1999.

II Michel Maffesoli, "The Return of the Tragic in Postmodern Societies", *NLH*, 35, 2005, 1, 133-49 and *Fleabag*, series 2, episode 6, created by Phoebe Waller-Bridge, 2018.

III Igor Shaitanov, "Aleksandr Veselovskii's Historical Poetics: Genre in Historical Poetics", *NLH*, 22, 2, 2001, 429-444 and *Good Omens*, episode one, created by Neil Gaiman, 2019.

IV Anis Bawarshi, "The Genre Function", *College English*, 62, 2, 2000, 335-60 and *The Parent Trap*, directed by Nancy Meyers, 1998.

Ralph Cohen defines genre as follows:

> A genre is a group (or groups) of texts historically characterized by components in interaction toward some general purpose containing features that are intertextual, the whole forming an identity that can become a subgenre

or can be the source of new genres. Genres occur in every language and many cross national borders. They are procedures for organizing knowledge and communicating it. They express our thoughts, feelings, and actions with regard to that knowledge (Rowlett, 184).

Cohen emphasizes that his genre theory is not subject to rules or laws but capable of modifications or radical changes desired by the author or artist. The modifications, according to Cohen, range from variation to innovation, from evolutionary change to radical alteration. Distinguishing variation from innovation involves meticulous attention to the details of the work of art rather than reference to generic rules or laws. Genres, as conceived by Cohen, are always changing; each new version of a genre alters the genre. For example, Eliot's *The Love Song of J. Alfred Prufrock* (1915) when seen as a dramatic monologue, a genre most familiar to us in Robert Browning's *My Last Duchess* (1842), alters the genre. Most of Browning's dramatic monologues play on the irony of the speaker inadvertently revealing something much more negative about himself than is intended. Presenting himself as the wronged husband, the Duke, the speaker of *My Last Duchess*, reveals to us that he has done a terrible injustice to the Duchess. The irony in Eliot's poem is of a different sort: Prufrock's dramatic monologue about failed love is, in fact, true to its title, a love song. Eliot adds a new dimension to the genre, suggesting that a lament about the inability to love can be a form of love, moving the dramatic monologue somewhat closer to the love lyric.

The literary historian will need to decide if this change Eliot has made to the dramatic monologue is a variation or an innovation. In either case, the shared assumption is that genres do not remain constant but are subject to historical development. Although all genres have constraints that enable us to distinguish a dramatic monologue from a love lyric, a novel from a biography, a pastoral from a descriptive nature poem, this chapter will illustrate how genre allows for the modification of even the most basic constraints and permits expression of the limitations of genre.

I) Teresa de Lauretis, "Becoming Inorganic", *Critical Inquiry*, 29, 4, 2003 (CI) and David Cronenberg's *eXistenZ*, 1999.

Teresa de Lauretis analyses David Cronenberg's film *eXistenZ* by means of a genre of science fiction she calls "novum", a term she describes as follows:

> A novum or cognitive innovation is a totalizing phenomenon or relationship deviating from the author's and implied reader's norm of reality. Now no doubt, each and every poetic metaphor is a novum, while modern prose fiction has made new insights into man its rallying cry. However, though valid SF has deep affinities with poetry and innovative realistic fiction, by 'totalizing' I mean a novelty entailing a change of the whole universe of the tale (*CI*, 547).

The new generic term "novum SF" enables de Lauretis to address the totalizing elements of the film *eXistenZ*. I begin with an analysis of this film because it focuses on interactive virtual reality computer games: in fact, as de Lauretis remarks, the film is a game of games and thus provides a suitable introduction to the twenty-first century when this new form of entertainment—perhaps a new or super-genre—becomes an important phenomenon involving millions of players and billions of dollars. Indeed, a fifteen-year-old boy recently won almost £1,000,000, his portion of the second place prize at the international computer games cup. Notice that this generic term, "novum SF", points to the fact that two separate entities, computer games and existence or *eXistenZ* have here been combined—in that games in this film completely consume the lives of the players—representing a new genre or kind of film, certainly not circumscribed by any law or rule of computer games or SF genres. The basic distinction between player and game, between SF fantasy and reality, has been violated.

The key element of the film that the term "novum SF" refers to is games within games, or what in literary analyses are called "mises en abyme". At the end of the film when the main characters are asked whether or not they are still in the game(s), no reply is given: the implication is that games comprise all of existence, or that these players are no longer able to distinguish reality from a game. Although for de Lauretis this totalizing effect is primarily mental or psychological, it nonetheless also relates to the physical or somatic element of the movie. Instead of using a keyboard or joystick, the players physically attach themselves to their computers by way of ports for computer cables that are surgically inserted into their spines: these "umbycords" permit their entire being to participate in the game—a suitable emblem of the current obsession with interactive virtual reality computer games. An analysis of this film is a beginning for the present study because these "umbycords" literally represent how one genre moves beyond itself to combine with another genre—gamer and game combined—suggesting how genres can exceed what in the past seemed to be their limit.

The generic term "novum SF" enables de Lauretis to isolate the novel quality of this game genre, in Cohen's terms, a change in the genre that is an innovation, since the game differs from others in that the gamer is one with the game. Identification of this new genre offers De Lauretis a key to the artistic purpose of the film. She sees this new element in Freudian terms as related to the death drive. Near the end of his life in the 1920s, Freud came to believe that Eros, or the will to live, was accompanied by a death wish, and that these two opposing drives together form a basic element of humanity, dialectically related impulses that are embedded in our psyche. The win/lose element of the computer game seems to de Lauretis to appeal to these basic human drives.

While this interpretation is interesting and compelling, I want to focus on the function of genre as applied to *eXistenZ*. One commentator on the film calls it "ooey and gooey" because of all the vivid details concerning the attachment of computer cables by way of "umbycords" into human "ports" that require lubrication and therefore ooze. In my view, the function of the graphic visualisation of this minor surgery prepares us for the conclusion of the film when, by implication, the genre, in a sense, itself oozes out of the game genre, pointing to a world beyond the virtual computer realm. De Lauretis is of two minds about this border territory between virtual and real reality:

> I ... am ambivalent with and against my reading of Cronenberg's film. I want to recover Freud's doubt that a material reality does exist beyond our will to know, a material reality that is other in the sense that, like *Trieb* (drive), it is only ever available to us through its psychic effects, which are themselves, for the most part, material and embodied; for these would not be possible without it. As the world again grows darker in these times, I return to Freud's figuration of an unconscious death drive because it conveys the sense and the force of something in human reality that resists discursive articulation as well as political diplomacy, an otherness that haunts the dream of a common world (*CI*, 570).

For de Lauretis, Freud gives us an inkling of this other world, if it exists, by way of his theory of the death wish, but for my purposes, the means of access to that idea in the film is a function of the "novum SF" genre that draws us beyond the world of ordinary computer games. One reason that genres are not subject to laws and rules is that they change and adapt to the purpose of the artist or writer, or, in this case, the filmmaker. This particular genre exemplifies its deconstructive capacity; the totality of the virtual world of *eXistenZ* is subverted, oozing out into something beyond the game arena, whether we decide to call it reality, the human psyche, another game, or the death drive. And even if the final realm is seen as another game, it must be understood as different in kind from the games played by "umbycord" in the film.

This notion of genre as a leaky vessel helps explain that although not subject to laws or rules it is marked by some constraints: "novum SF" is a genre of games that goes beyond ordinary computer games but is still identifiable as a game genre. Flexibility of genre is not only available to the creator but also to the interpreter. For example a generic alternative reading to that of de Lauretis modifying somewhat her concept of the film as a Freudian "novum SF" could characterise *eXistenZ* as a mechanical/technological alternative to the time before personal computers when people played games without the need for "bioport" surgery connecting players to a machine. Such a view could involve a generic alternative: in place of de Lauretis' psycho-drama of the death wish, we would have an elegiac "novum SF" mourning the loss of the pre-computer game world.

Another reason that genres cannot be characterised by rules or laws is that they are historically bound, both for the writer or creator and for the reader or responder. In fact, de Lauretis' "novum SF" reading of *eXistenZ* is based upon an historical element different from the one I have suggested about the days before personal computers, an account of the rise of the idea of the death wish. In the early twentieth century, a student and former patient of Jung who became involved in a love relationship with him sought the help of Freud to end the liaison. In 1912, while still involved with Jung, Sabina Spielrein wrote a paper entitled "Destruction as Cause of Becoming", an early and perhaps the first published description of the death wish. This important psychological innovation was largely ignored by her two rival mentors, who were vying with one another for her affection and respect. Eventually, Freud recognised the importance of her innovation, but Spielrein's contribution has remained insufficiently recognised. De Lauretis explains:

> Caught between the two men in their oedipal rivalry, Spielrein never acquired a name in psychoanalytic theory, although she was a medical doctor, a practicing and training analyst (of Jean Piaget, among others), and the author of significant papers on female creativity and language symbolism, including one on child language development that anticipated the arguments of Melanie Klein and Julia Kristeva. She eventually married a Jewish doctor, had two children, and moved back to the Soviet Union in 1923, where she started and ran a children's clinic until Stalin outlawed psychoanalysis in 1936. Very little is known about her life after this point, but she is believed to have died in the holocaust. She never had a chance. Today we know her only as another egregious product of the old technology of gender. However, the idea sketched out in her paper was not only not Jung's idea, as Freud had suspected, but proved to be central to Freud's later conception of the death drive and, as we shall see, may still have a bearing on the new technologies of gender in our time (*CI*, 551).

This sad story of the neglect of a brilliant woman's important contribution to psychoanalysis provides a basis for de Lauretis' choice of what might be called psycho- or Freudian-novum SF as the genre of *eXistenZ*. A victim of "the old technology of gender", Spielrein provides us, according to de Lauretis, with ideas that bear upon "the new technologies of gender in our time". The suggestion is that, like the gamers in the film, Jung and Freud became so obsessed with winning the game of vying for Spielrein's affection that they completely neglected Spielrein's essay on the death wish, a key concept of psychoanalysis. (Thanks to Dr. Alexis Tomarken, I was made aware of a film about the relationship of Sabina Spielrein with Freud and Jung, entitled *A Dangerous Method*, 2011, directed by David Cronenberg, and starring Keira Knightley.)

De Lauretis' analysis makes clear that genre is a two-way street, used by the author/creator to present the work of art and by the audience/critic as a means of interpretation. Throughout history the audience/critic may change the genre of interpretation, as a part of James Joyce's *Ulysses* was reinterpreted as a drama, *Ulysses in Nighttown*. De Lauretis believes that the present technologies of sex change give an added dimension to Freud's death drive; this impulse that in the early twentieth century was seen exclusively in psychological terms has now, as *eXistenZ* displays so graphically, a new physical dimension—that of sex change—that may even be suggested by this peculiar title, implying perhaps that the X/Y sexual chromosome distinction may be replaced by a Z for unknown, neither exclusively male nor female or even both. The critical choice between psycho-novum SF and elegiac-novum SF is a historical/interpretive one, a decision about how the work speaks to our time. The historical nature of genre is continually emphasized in Cohen's conception for a number of reasons. As we have seen, genres themselves change in history. Also, generic flexibility enables creators like Cronenberg to push the boundaries beyond their old limits, physically connecting game and gamers as well as interpreters like de Lauretis who see the film in Freudian terms connecting present-day feminism with the dilemma of Sabina Spielrein in the early twentieth century. In the next section, we shall see that the hierarchy of genres is also affected by history.

II) Michel Maffesoli, "The Return of the Tragic in Postmodern Societies", *NLH*, 35, 1, 2004, 133-49 and *Fleabag*, series 2, episode 6, 2019.

Cohen explains that the grouping of genres or generic hierarchies is also historical:

> Genre writing—of whatever kind—is historical in the sense that at a particular time certain works are identified as belonging together by an author or critic. And this grouping is made to relate such writing to literary, social, or other ends. When such writings become unimportant, the writing of a particular genre diminishes and is discontinued while other genres assume importance. Thus in the Renaissance serious objections arose to including *De rerum natura* in the genre 'poetry,' but during the restoration and eighteenth-century Lucretius' georgic poem becomes once again an important literary genre and thus is included in the comprehensive genre 'poetry' (Rowlett, 100).

More specifically, genres are historical by their very nature because for Cohen they are always involved in a hierarchy that is a function of the social ties of the historical era:

> At any moment in literary history there exists a particular system of genres with social ties ... Every genre hierarchy which actually exists is characterized by a norm of combination ... These modes of combination ... that appear in books of proverbs, or in sonnets, or in odes, or in dramas, or in epics ... are governed by underlying principles of the combination of features (Rowlett, 43).

What Cohen means by genre combinations is explained as follows, a topic to be pursued in more detail in the next chapter:

> The combinatory nature of genres moves in our time to mixtures of media and to mixtures resulting from the electronic world in which we live. Films, TV genres, university educational programs, our very explanations of identity and discourses all indicate combinations of one kind or another. The precise nature of these combinations differ, but what genre theorists and critics can now study are the interactions within combinations and how these differ from earlier combinations, whether in epic, tragedy, novel, lyric, etc. (Rowlett, 111).

In an essay translated into English in 2004 from a work originally published in French in 2000, Michel Maffesoli asserts that we are at the present stage of postmodernity in a new age of tragedy, a position based upon what Cohen calls "social ties", resulting in tragedy being at the top of the genre hierarchy. Maffesoli explains:

> The great paradigm shift that is taking place ... is indeed the slippage from an 'ego-centered' to a 'place-centered' ... worldview. In the former instance of modernity that is now ending, primacy is given to the rational individual living in a contractual society. In the latter instance of an emerging postmodernity, it is groups that come into play, 'neotribes' that lay siege to specific spaces and harmonize with them. In the drama of modernity one finds an optimistic claim to totality of the self, the world, the state. In the tragedy of postmodernity there is a concern for entirety leading to the loss of the individual ego in a greater self of natural or social otherness (*NLH*, 35, 1,134).

This postmodern conception of the self is seen, according to Maffesoli, in the daily newspaper accounts of the young in our society:

> We often see commentators puzzling over the violent character of some news item, taking note of the suicide of an adolescent seeking to emulate the rock singer who was his model. But this is not at all surprising. Such excessive action reveals a latent state of mind that sees in paroxysmal revolt, in a death that is really enacted, the only alternative to a sanitized existence where the certainty of dying is countered by the certainty of dying of boredom. Hard rock in its various forms, decadent styles in painting and dress, in short the nomadism that is around us, all reveal the return of the barbarians inside our gates, that is to say, the bursting apart of the civilized universe that modernity, over the course of three centuries, has patiently established (*NLH*, 35, 1, 136).

But the tragic world that Maffesoli describes is one that is without melodrama, a mundane world of unacknowledged fatalism: "there is little talk of all this in the organs of established thought. Denial is mandatory; we dare not speak of what frightens us. ... it is a deafening unsaid, for if there is anything that is lived empirically on a day-to-day basis, it is indeed 'the tragic sense of life'" (*NLH*, 35, 1, 133).

Daily life for Maffesoli is filled with group endeavours and activities that result in the neglect of individuality, so much so that what you become as a person is not the result of inner drives and ambitions but of outward circumstances: "huge rallies, crowds of all kinds, collective trances, fusion through sport, ecstasy through music, religious or cultural effervescences, all raise the individual up to a form of plenitude that is not provided by the greyness of economic or political functionality. In all of this there is a kind of magical participation in what is foreign, in a globality that transcends the singularity of the individual" (*NLH*, 35,1, 142-3). The result of this pervasive world of tragedy without sadness or one so inured to sadness that it is as commonplace as the weather is that "ever greater numbers of individuals [are] eager to perfect themselves through religion, fusion with nature, or merging with the group" (*NLH*, 35, 1, 146).

Here we are reminded of the priest (David Scott) in the final episode of *Fleabag*, series 2. He sleeps with Fleabag (Phoebe Waller-Bridge), experiences bouts of uncontrollable passion, kissing her passionately in public, and finally admits to loving her. Yet when she also confesses her love for him, he replies, "It will pass." For her part, Fleabag accepts his decision to let their love fade away as she accepts the other disappointments of her life, the refusal of a bank loan for her shop, a future mother-in-law from hell, a brother-in-law who tries to seduce her. This particular episode focuses on the marriage ceremony of Fleabag's father (Bill Paterson), now a widower, and her godmother (Olivia Colman), whose smile resembles the snarl of a gorilla. Understandably, when the marriage is imminent the groom retreats to the attic where he is rescued by Fleabag who with characteristic fatalism helps her father recover his nerve, enabling him to reappear at the ceremony that she and her sister have been dreading.

After the marriage vows are completed, the priest remarks, looking pointedly at Fleabag, that love is painful, indeed, a form of agony ordained by God. Fleabag, however, is at that moment thinking about her sister Claire (Sian Clifford) who, in a previous scene, by kneeling and begging, has convinced her husband to agree to a divorce. During the priest's closing remarks near the end of the ceremony, Fleabag points her sister to a discreet means of leaving the wedding to join her new lover. Nonetheless, the relationship between the siblings provides little consolation for their problems. In an exchange between the two sisters when Fleabag suggests they could just be friends, Claire responds, "I'm your sister, get your own friends."

But while Fleabag more than understands the pain of love, she is not simply the passive martyr. She tells Claire about the sexual advances of her husband, steals the statue from her own godmother, and has a reputation for one-night stands. In fact, as a final insult to her soon-to-be stepmother, she gives the statue to her as a wedding present, only to be told that the statue was modelled on her mother. So Fleabag steals it back again. At the end of the episode when the priest leaves her—perhaps for the last time—she holds the statue that she had despised because it was made by her stepmother but now treasures because it is modelled after her mother. This final poignant moment is one of the few times we see Fleabag on her own; for the most part she is with groups interacting in ways that, as Maffesoli predicted, attend to the interests and problems of others rather than her private and individual concerns. Even in intimate moments with Claire or the priest, Fleabag focuses on their concerns, from Claire's problems with her husband to the priest's obsession with squirrels.

But so far my account leaves out all the laughs, and the programme was a roaring success because of the humour, particularly that of Fleabag, whose most original and characteristic kind of comedy involves her frequent over-the-shoulder glances at the audience. The general affect of this breaking of the fourth wall that separates the audience from the actors is to present herself as having one foot in the TV/play and one in the audience, which in addition to its comic function also reminds us that she is the writer/creator of the show. By this means, it seems to me, Fleabag renders her tragic situation as ordinary, no different from that of the rest of us, and her wonderfully expressive eyes suggest that she is laughing at herself and what she has created as much as we are. Perhaps the quintessential moment when she is at her most humorous and self-denigrating, refusing to consider herself as tragic, is when at a public Quaker-like meeting where one is expected to be deeply honest, she stands tentatively suggesting, "I was just wondering, if I had bigger tits would I still be a feminist." The nature of the humour is difficult to define; there is sadness, so sad that one had better laugh and get on with life. But our laughter stems from living in Maffesoli's tragic world permitting us to enjoy and appreciate the humour, and from the fact that, at least since Shakespeare, tragedy can include comedy. In either case, the genre, comic tragedy, is indicated by Fleabag's glances at the audience. If Maffesoli is correct, the hierarchy of genres has changed, with comic-tragedy more prevalent in our time than sheer comedy because of the social situation of our time, an age, as we have seen in the previous section, marked by the death wish.

The present predominance of tragedy is also clear in *The Lehman Trilogy* (2018), directed by Sam Mendes, a movie of a drama performed on stage in London that could also be viewed at local cinemas. This new radical of presentation—cinema and drama—lends a certain immediacy to this historical drama: although a story of the past, the action of the play is, in a sense, still being played out before us on stage. The story of the demise of the family-owned investment bank that went bankrupt in 2008, one of the key factors in the fiscal crisis of that year, presents itself, as Maffesoli led us to expect, as merely history: we are shown the journey to success of the first of three brothers who emigrated from Germany to the USA with a single suitcase and almost no money. Eventually, Henry ends up opening a tiny dry goods store in Montgomery, Alabama, where he is eventually joined by his two brothers. As a result of a huge cotton fire in the area, they begin to buy and sell cotton, eventually amassing a small fortune and opening a second office in New York City.

Their sons and grandsons use this fortune to form the investment bank that makes them all millionaires, then billionaires.

The final and fatal phase occurs when the bank changes its policy from commodity transactions based upon products, cotton, coffee, and others, to unsecured loans and bad mortgages, as did so many other banks of the day. But they were among the first to come unstuck. The shift from investment in real products to risky mortgages leads to their downfall, a truly Marxist case history, where the intrinsic value of an object is converted by the market into a commodity value of exchange, reminiscent of the famous table in *Capital,* which begins to spin and dance when subject to market forces that no longer care if it functions as a table or has any other use except to be the occasion for the exchange of money.

But many other banks behaved similarly and yet still thrive today. One is left with the question, is the Lehman story tragic or merely a historical microcosm, rather like the story of Richard Nixon, who declared in the end that he was being punished for what was considered normal behaviour by other politicians. The cinema-play provides a generic clue to the answer to this question. The theatrical set never changes from the Lehman brothers' New York office (albeit with minor decorative additions) and the cast is restricted to the three brothers, Henry, Emmanuel, and Meyer, played by Simon Russell Beale, Ben Miles, and Adam Godley, respectively, who between them take on all parts in the three-hour drama, including those of grandchildren and women.

For the audience all the action takes place in the office/home; the genre of a domestic tragedy that always remains within the family home/office suggests isolation from the outside world, an understandable response from a Jewish family in a world that excluded and persecuted them for their religion. But while other banks such as Barclay's diversified and maintained ordinary client services in addition to investments and thereby survived (although just barely in some cases), Lehman's was the fourth largest of the exclusively investment banks. It is important to keep in mind that while this version of the history of Lehman brothers implies that the Lehman family managed the bank until its demise, no member of the Lehman family was in fact involved with the bank after 1969. Sam Mendes presents the Lehman Brothers' business failure as an exclusively family affair, a presentation that involves some poetic license but suits the genre of family tragedy.

An indication of Mendes' position was provided by an element that is unique to this new genre. In one of the intermissions, the audience is introduced to the pianist and the composer of the background music. Their comments make clear that the director decided to use only piano music imbued with motifs from the melodies common to the culture of nineteenth-century Bavaria, the region where the three Lehman brothers were born and grew up. The solo piano is understood in the context of the play as rather dated in early twentieth-century United States: one of the younger generation of Lehmans remarks that the preferred modern instrument is the violin because, unlike the piano, it shows a better profile of the player. Mendes' basso continuo of old Bavaria reminds us of the family's roots and that, however modernised the setting, the family origin remains at the heart of the tragedy.

Our present historical perspective on the financial crisis of 2008 is an important factor in deciding what lens we use to view this historical event of the recent past. As Maffesoli suggests, our culture presents us with generic choices. *The Lehman Trilogy* can be seen as tragic in that insulated by great wealth the Lehmans were unable to contemplate the possibility of normal, everyday failure. Alternatively, the Lehmans may be viewed as the tragic victims of the tribalism that Maffesoli sees as the mark of our age and that enabled them paradoxically both to amass the fortune and then to lose it. Instead of laws and rules, the tragic genre offers a number of interpretive possibilities. But it is the mark of our age, according to Maffesoli, that it is a tragedy rather than, say, a tale of fraudulent financiers.

Many may be troubled by the notion of the fall of Lehman

brothers bank as tragic, particularly given the liberties taken with regard to the fact that the Lehmans ended their relationship with the bank in 1969, but Sam Mendes' version of events nonetheless presents the story as a family tragedy. So while genres are themselves subject to history and purveyors of history, they are not completely limited by history. Art is a kind of negotiation with history; in a period when tragedy is at the top of the generic hierarchy, Sam Mendes is able to take some liberties with the facts to present *The Lehman Trilogy* as a domestic tragedy. And, once again, the genre is flexible enough to permit these liberties for purposes of artistic goals. In the next section, I consider formalism, an alternative to genre that, in my view, neglects artistic purpose.

III) Igor Shaitanov, "Aleksandr Veselovskii's Historical Poetics: Genre in Historical Poetics", *NLH*, 32, 2, 2001, 429-44 and *Good Omens*, episode one, 2019.

In this third section, I wish to demonstrate how the open or flexible quality of genre helps avoid the formal constraints of formalism. Igor Shaitanov demonstrates that the Russian formalists, including Vladimir Propp, Mikhail Bakhtin, Yury Tynyanov, Viktor Shlovskii, and others, are not formalists as the term is used to describe the new critics of the United States. Instead, these Russian critics are all influenced by the "historical poetics" of Aleksandr Veselovskii whose position is, according to Shaitanov, a historicised version of genre criticism. The misunderstanding began when "a naïve logic from the formalists' precedence encouraged a tendency to enlist each Russian theoretician … as another formalist." But more careful analysis reveals a different story: "time passed before a simple truth was revealed: that Propp could be classified as a formalist in a very loose sense, while Bakhtin remained the staunch opponent, who as early as 1924 rejected the formal method as a 'material aesthetics' and dubbed its creators 'specificators' " (*NLH*, 32, 2,

429). This more accurate understanding of the Russian theorists highlights Veselovskii's notion of "historical poetics", and almost all of those so-called Russian formalists show clearly the influence of this concept in their theories.

The problem is that Veselovskii's project was never finished: "aesthetic critics believed that Veselovskii underestimated the artistic quality of literature ... and marxists found that he failed to understand historical determinism ... they advanced a different point of view, 'new form comes about in order not to express new content but in order to replace an old form that has already lost its artistic viability'" (*NLH*, 431-2). Shaitanov explains that Veselovskii never completed his theory because he insisted on an inductive method that derived principles from practice. Near the end of his life, he became hopelessly bogged down in careful historical analyses.

Nevertheless, Veselovskii freed criticism from the romantic singular focus on the author rather than the work, and all the Russian theorists who followed after Veselovskii attributed to him the idea of the function of genre. Shaitanov concludes:

> Like many other contemporary schools, historical poetics encourages one to concentrate on the word and text, but, unlike most modern textual approaches, historical poetics historicises its subject when it engages itself not with the word in the text (after the long practices of new criticism) but with the word in the genre (*NLH*, 442).

Shaitanov is arguing that the text cannot be understood without a context and that genre is the most fruitful context because it is historical.

I turn now to *Good Omens*, episode one, in order to demonstrate the difference between a formalist or new critical reading and a generic one. This first episode introduces us to the two main characters, the angel and the demon, Michael Sheen as Aziraphale and David Tennant as Crawley, later Crowley, the serpent who tempts Eve. Representatives of heaven and hell on earth for six thousand years, they have become friends of sorts—Aziraphale says he really doesn't like Crowley but regularly enjoys meals and endures car rides with him.

The dilemma of this episode is that the Antichrist is about to be born and the demon and angel have been given instructions by their authorities to help bring about Armageddon. But enjoying life on earth, recognising that the most likely result of the plans from their superiors from above and below will be the end of all earthly life, they decide together to try to prevent war between Heaven and Hell. However, to achieve peace between the warring parties, they will have to disobey or at least mislead their respective higher authorities. Understandably, Crowley has little trouble reconciling himself to this deception, although at considerable risk from some particularly vicious devils who relish his downfall. Aziraphale, as we would expect, finds these means highly distasteful although necessary. But they have a stroke of good luck. The plan to place the Antichrist child with the family of the US ambassador—on the assumption that he will be free to develop his naturally evil disposition—is thwarted by an accident.

The chattering order of St Beryl, satanic nuns entrusted with placing the child, inadvertently choose the wrong household. The Antichrist is sent to an ordinary middle-class family in Swindon, is named—not to say christened—Adam (Daniel Mays), and becomes a normal boy, if a bit controlling with his friends. The mistake is only revealed to the higher and lower authorities when the hellhound is to appear to the Antichrist to lead him toward Armageddon. But upon seeing Adam the hellhound miraculously morphs into what Adam wants it to be, a lovely, playful puppy, a companion for the growing boy and his friends.

The comedy involves for the most part the good and bad angel out-smarting the higher and lower forces of good and evil because they both understand the ways of earth. For instance, in the beginning of this episode after Crowley, who changes his name to Crowley in order to sound less snake-like and more human, has tempted Eve, we hear the conversation of the good and bad angels, both perched on a wall above Eden witnessing the expulsion of Adam and Eve. Remarking on the eating of the apple, Crowley says, "That went down like a lead balloon," an expression of contempt for the higher (or lower) authorities who mete out this punishment to the first humans. In tacit agreement with Crowley's criticism of the harsh treatment of Adam and Eve, Aziraphale gives Adam and Eve his sword of fire to guide and protect them in the wilderness of the fallen world that has become their new environment.

One possible formalist reading of this episode would be to view it as a satire of religion, ranging from the Fall to Armageddon. But the dark comedy of the episode does not attack all forms of religion, particularly since the two protagonists are angels. By contrast, I would suggest a generic reading that could see the episode as an example of the mock-heroic where the authority figures, in this instance, the angels above and below, have become, in our time, not saviours but impediments to peace and happiness. The mock-heroic as a genre is not directed at the heroic figures of the past—the ancient biblical figures of earth and heaven—but to the modern equivalents who constitute a mockery of ancient heroism.

The use of the mock-heroic genre in a religious context goes back at least to the 1960s *Beyond the Fringe* revue when a group of doomsday cultists await the end of the world. On the appointed day, when nothing happens, they disperse disappointed, the leader remarking, "Well, it's not quite the conflagration I'd been banking on." In 1969, Monty Python's *Life of Brian* appeared. This very popular film is about Brian Cohen, a neighbour of Jesus Christ, who is mistaken for Christ. Brian's crucifixion is accompanied by the now famous song, "Look on the Bright Side". Although some religious figures regarded the film as blasphemous, most took it with good humour, and it was a big box office success in Great Britain and the USA. The point of both satires is not against religion per se. The *Beyond the Fringe* sketch satirizes literalists who believe that they can set an exact date for the end of the world, when, as their leader explains, "the veil of the Temple will be rent in twain". (In Chapter Three, we shall see that the third episode of *Good Omens* is making a similar point.) *Life of Brian* substitutes an ordinary man for Christ—as his mother points out, "he is not the Messiah; he is a very naughty boy"—to suggest how modern messiahs are very pale imitations of the original Saviour.

Good Omens, in my view, continues in this genre. Concerning what Cohen calls "social ties", this generic choice would point to the contrasting warring figures of heaven and hell as representing the extreme forms of religion or religiosity that exploit religion to justify the harming of innocents, another example of Maffesoli's tragic outlook on the present. Instead of religious satire, the mock-heroic points to the corruption of the religious establishments that use and abuse religion for purposes of power. By contrast, the spirituality of religion is seen in the friendship and behaviour of Crowley and Aziraphale, whose acts of human decency are thwarted and disapproved of by all the other "superior" demons and angels.

Even the supposed Antichrist, as his name Adam Young (Sam Taylor Buck) suggests, is a high-spirited, well-meaning young boy. The "hellhound" responds to Adam's normality, morphing into "Dog", as named by Adam. In short, the Antichrist when raised by decent people in a normal household turns out to be nothing like the "warlock" the religious establishment intended him to become: the humane spirit of the earth—the love of his parents—has prevailed over the evil plans for Armageddon.

The advantage of the generic reading is that it places *Good Omens* in literary history as a version of the mock-heroic, and in social and political history suggesting how pseudo-religion or religion as political power pervades the ideological and physical wars of our time. Genre criticism thus moves beyond the superficial formalist satire of religion; the angel and demon on earth represent more of genuine religion than either of the power brokers in heaven or hell. And Maffesoli could well claim that the premise that many forms of present-day religion are not truly religious is another aspect of our tragic age, although presented in non-melodramatic terms, as history in *The Lehman Trilogy,* and as dark comedy in *Fleabag* and *Good Omens.* But the flexibility of genre has its limitations; ideology conveyed in a genre is not, Cohen argues, a function of genre but of the ideologist, the subject of the next section.

IV) Anis Bawarshi, "The Function of Genre", *College English*, (CE), 62, 3, 2000, 335-360 and *The Parent Trap*, directed by Nancy Meyers, 1998.

Anis Bawarshi argues persuasively that genre functions not merely in literature and literary analysis but also in other kinds of linguistic actions:

> I hope to expose the extent to which genres are constitutive both of literary and nonliterary (con)texts as well as of literary and nonliterary writers and readers. … Central to this genre-based inquiry are such questions as how and why texts as cultural artifacts are produced; how they in turn reflect and help enact social actions; and how, finally, they can serve as sites for cultural critique and change. Genres, I argue, can and should serve as the sites for such inquiry because genres, ultimately, are the rhetorical environments within which we recognize,

enact, and consequently reproduce various situations, practices, relations, and identities (*CE*, 346).

Bawarshi proposes to "democratize" Foucault's "author-function" by extending it beyond literature to any rhetorical situation, what he calls "genre function". Since the "author-function" for Bawarshi involves ideological assumptions, genre is a more inclusive term that avoids the elitism of the notion of the author.

> In fact, it is quite possible that the author-function is itself a function of literary genres, which create the ideological conditions that give rise to this subject we call an 'author.' and so, I propose to subsume what Foucault calls the author-function within what I am calling the genre function, which constitutes all discourses' and all writers' modes of existence, circulation, and functioning within a society, whether the writer is William Shakespeare or a student in a first-year writing course, and whether the text is a sonnet or a first-year student theme (*CE*, 345).

Genres, for Bawarshi, have therefore a significant function in society as both regulatory and constitutive: in addition to regulating communication and interpretation, genre is seen as a force in history that has an effect upon history. He formulates his position in the following terms:

> Genre does not simply regulate a preexisting social activity; instead, it constitutes the activity by making it possible through its ideological and rhetorical conventions. In fact, genre reproduces the activity by providing individuals with the conventions for enacting it. We perform an activity in terms of how we recognize

it, that is, how we identify and come to know it, and we recognize an activity by way of genre. Genre helps shape and enable our social actions by rhetorically constituting the way we recognize the situations within which we function (*CE*, 340).

Bawarshi therefore concludes that genres are not merely a means of communication but intimately bound up with how we learn and behave. In addition to aiding what we do when we communicate, genres help us organise, experience, and understand the act of communicating:

> Basically, genres shape us as we give shape to them, which is why they constitute our activities and regulate how and why we perform them. In this way, we can attribute to the genre function many of the claims Foucault makes for the author-function, except that the genre function accounts for all discursive activities, not just those endowed with a certain literary value (*CE*, 356).

While I believe Cohen would have little problem with extending genre beyond literature, Bawarshi's claims are so all-encompassing that we are left to wonder what is not genre. My view is that aesthetic genres differ from those of everyday communication in that they are marked by a more complex history and different aims. But for the present purpose I want to focus on the question of ideology and genre, a key element in Bawarshi's replacement of Foucault's "author-function" with "genre-function". Bawarshi's main argument is that all forms of language may have an ideological element that is not a function of the genre but of the aim of the author/speaker or the interpreter/listener. The following visual examples will serve to test this argument.

The Parent Trap is a good example of both genre and ideology. It is the story of identical twins, Annie and Hallie, separated at birth when the parents divorce. Each parent raises one child in separate countries, England and USA, without any direct contact between them for eleven years. The film begins when the twins, now nearly twelve years old, are accidentally sent to the same summer camp. Unaware of being sisters, they become natural rivals, then friends, finally discovering that they are related. Curious about the other parent they have never met, they decide at the end of camp to switch places, returning to the other sister's home, pretending to be one another. In California, Annie (Lindsay Lohan) discovers that her father Nick (Dennis Quaid) is engaged to marry a young woman who does not like or want to have children. So by way of furtive phone calls, the twins decide to prevent this new marriage by getting their parents together with the hope of renewing their marriage. Unsurprisingly, the film ends not only with the remarriage of the parents but also with the carers of the two girls, Chessy (Lisa Ann Walter) and Martin (Simon Kunz), who helped the girls with their "parent trap", becoming engaged. The turning point is when, asked by his fiancée to choose between herself and the girls, Nick decides emphatically in favour of his daughters.

The genre—we could call it family divorce romance—is designed to show that the children are at the heart of the family; not only does Nick choose the children over his fiancée but also the romance of Chessy and Martin derives from their utter devotion to the respective twins they raise. I expect that many of my former students would characterise the end of this film as "cheesy", that is, sentimental and contrived. There is very scant reason to believe that the parents, Nick and Liz (Natasha Richardson) have remained in love for over eleven years and their remarriage is mainly the result of the trickery of the twins.

Here we see the most overt ideological element of the film: family and children are valued over parental compatibility. Nick's fiancée is simply left out in the cold, and Chessy and Martin are rewarded with one another because of their love for the children. While the genre of this movie successfully conveys this message, the ideology of the message is not inherent in the genre itself. Consider another film of this genre, *Kramer versus Kramer* (1979) focusing on the same issue of marriage and divorce, parental incompatibility and the plight of the child. In this instance, the mother gives custody of her son to the father. But after some time when the boy and his father have formed a healthy and firm relationship, the mother sues to regain custody. To the disappointment of the father and son, the court awards custody of the boy to the mother. In the end when she comes to pick up her son, she recognises that he needs and loves his father. Instead of taking him from his father, she asks for a private moment with her son to say goodbye. As she prepares to say goodbye to her son, she turns in tears to her ex-husband to ask, "How do I look?" Her ex-husband answers, "Terrific." The ideological message here is very different from that of "The Parent Trap": the love that the parents share for their son is valued over any remnant of love between the adults. The bond between one parent and the child may be more important than the nuclear family.

In fact, ten years after *The Parent Trap*, Nancy Meyers directed a film entitled *It's Complicated* (2009), that further investigates the ideology of the family divorce comedy. In this film, starring Meryl Streep, Alec Baldwin, and Steve Martin, the divorcees have "an affair" with one another. Their three children, now young adults, are thoroughly confused, wavering as to whether or not they prefer their parents to remarry. In the end their mother (Meryl Streep) decides that instead of remarrying their father (Alec Baldwin) she will pursue her dating relationship with her architect (Steve Martin). We are left in doubt as to whether parental compatibility or the nuclear family is more important. In between *Kramer vs. Kramer*, 1979, the earliest instance of this sub-genre of children controlling or influencing marriage and the most recent, *It's Complicated*, 2009, is *Sleepless in Seattle*, 1993. In this film, the child influences his father away from one woman and toward another who then turns out to be more compatible with both the father and the son than the previous woman. The ideology here also occupies a middle ground between family love for the child and the love between the parents. But again, the genre accommodates different if not contradictory family ideologies. As Cohen argues, "a genre can be the site of contrary ideologies". Hence "if the same genre can be used antithetically, the attribution to it of a single ideology is untenable" (Rowlett, 118).

In conclusion, genre is not fettered by rules, laws, forms, or ideologies and is limited but not completely controlled by formal constraints and by history. Formed by and changing in history, genres facilitate communication and interpretation. Changing yet recognisably distinct from other genres, like members of a family, genres are pliable and resistant. They also exist in systems and hierarchies that are subject to history. The adaptability of genres to change enables them to be combined, both competitively and cooperatively: genre combination is the subject of the next chapter.

Chapter Two

Genre Combinations and Interpretation

I Dorothea von Mücke, "Profession/Confession", *NLH*, 34, 2, 257-74 and *The Boys*, Season 1, episode 6, developed by Eric Kripke, 2019.

II Elisabeth Bronfen, "Femme Fatale: Negotiations of Tragic Desire", *NLH*, 35, 1, 103-16 and *Bridget Jones's Baby*, directed by Sharon Maguire, 2017.

III Emily Apter, "Taskography: Translation as a Genre of Literary Labor", *PMLA*, 122, 5, 2007, 1403-13 and *Elementary*, season 5, episode 2, created by Robert Doherty, 2016.

Ralph Cohen believes that almost all genres appear in combination with other genres and that the mixture of genres is key to interpretation of the individual work of art and assessment of its place in history. The following passage was cited earlier but is worth repeating:

> The combinatory nature of genres moves in our time to mixtures of media and to mixtures resulting from the world in which we live. Films, TV dramas, university

educational programs, our very explanations of identity and discourses all indicate combinations of one kind or another. The precise nature of these combinations differ, but what genre critics and theorists can now study are the interactions within combinations and how these differ from earlier combinations, whether in epic, tragedy, novel, lyric, etc. (Rowlett, 111).

But Cohen warns at the outset that generic combinations are not necessarily without contradiction and dissonance:

Combinations in no way imply harmony. The constituents of a genre can come in conflict, as Hamlet's discourse of revenge conflicts with his later discourse of peace and fate. Such clashes are only one of the interrelations that can occur in a text. One can observe the elevation or domination of one genre by another, when, for example, ballads become part of the ballad opera or when, in *A Portrait of the Artist*, a dialogue on aesthetics provides the grounds for understanding the narrative structure (Rowlett, 160).

In addition to aiding in the analysis of the work itself, mixtures of genres—whether harmonious or disharmonious—enable us to refine our understanding of historical development and to place the work in the historical continuum:

Genre criticism, as I propose it, challenges the received view of historical change. Change remains problematic because we are only beginning to recognize the importance of genre theory in formulating its problems. Genre theory provides formulations for change by stipulating constituents of a text within a genre. Thus it becomes possible to note the particulars of a change and what these imply in relation to aims (Rowlett, 149).

But perhaps the most important element of generic combination, for Cohen, is that it is itself a form of interpretation. Finally and most importantly, genre combinations represent interpretations that the critic must not avoid; "for a critic or historian to disregard the relation of the ballad to tragedy in interpreting *The London Merchant* is to ignore the complicated process of generic and historical change and the fact that the tragedy is an interpretation" (Rowlett, 304). The choice on the part of the creator of a work of art to combine genres is an interpretive decision and therefore crucial to interpretive analysis.

I) Dorothea von Mücke, "Profession / Confession", *NLH*, 34, 2, 257-74 and *The Boys*, episode 6, 2019.

In an issue of *New Literary History* (34, 2, 2003) edited by Ralph Cohen and Hayden White, Cohen explains Dorothea von Mücke's essay as follows:

> Accepting Bakhtin's belief in the evolution 'of nonliterary speech genres into literary genres …' von Mücke selects a nonliterary segment from Rousseau's *Emile, ou, de l'Education* (1762) entitled "Profession of Faith of a Savoyard Vicar"… arguing that in the novel this formalized profession becomes a secular personal literary statement… [by revealing] an aesthetic dimension (*NLH*, 34, 2, xi).

This aesthetic dimension involves literary history and interpretation. Von Mücke begins by pointing out that a profession of faith can take two forms, a recitation of a prescribed credo, usually a religious formula, or a personal statement of belief. In the period when Rousseau was writing this difference was very significant. Authorities of the French Catholic Church were scandalised, to Rousseau's surprise, by the use of a statement of faith in *Emile* that departed from or omitted elements of the Nicene Creed. In this respect *Emile* is a historical document since Rousseau asserted that the faith of the Vicar of Savoy was similar to his own profession of faith as presented earlier in his letters and other writings. One reason for this negative response on the part of some clergymen—von Mücke tells us that the book was publicly burned in Paris and Geneva—is that, unlike Rousseau, the Vicar of Savoy is a man of the cloth and as such likely to convey more religious authority. Here the literary and historical merge in that the fictional character of the vicar renders this new kind of credo more threatening to the authorities because it reaches a wider, secular audience and gives a clerical cloak, however fictional, to the doctrine. This mixture of historical and literary genres highlights what von Mücke calls the rise of "modern subjectivity", the development from ritualised credo to individualised profession of faith.

In addition, this genre combination has formal and structural significance that von Mücke shows to be related to interpretation. She begins with Bakhtin's notion that literary genres, although derived from speech genres, are "played out" in a literary structure. The traditional speech act profession of faith is spoken by the person professing faith and assumed to be truthful as opposed to the fictional possibility inherent in a literary genre. Rousseau, according to von Mücke, makes the transition from speech to literary genre, Rousseau's concrete form of Bakhtin's "playing out". "The concept of 'playing out' suggests that the pragmatic dimension of ordinary speech genres within a literary work is not fully actualised but instead highlighted only in its pragmatic potential" (*NLH*, 34, 2, 259). "Playing out" for von Mücke means placing language from ordinary speech in a new, literary context. The Vicar of Savoy, a tutor and friend of Rousseau in real life, agrees to speak to Emile about his religious belief.

Preparing the reader for the conversation between the vicar and Emile, the narrator begins by eliminating the possibility that Emile was drawn to religion because of a problem about his own faith.

> Although the Savoyard Vicar does not directly belong to Emile's universe, to the extent that he is introduced and fleshed out as a character who was a crucial figure to Emile's tutor, he clearly belongs to that aspect of the *Emile* that makes the book something different from a mere pedagogical treatise; that might not quite justify calling the *Emile* an educational novel, but that consists in Rousseau's strategy to provide his reader with concrete examples and hypothetical experiments that have the status of simulations of lived experience rather than merely dry theory (*NLH*, 34, 2, 262).

In fact, von Mücke points out that up to this point in the narrative Emile has been deliberately guided away from religion to avoid "breeding fanaticism and prejudice". And the profession of faith is not even a part of the education of Emile; it is located at the end of his education, just before his tutor inspires him with the idea of the ideal woman. Nevertheless, Rousseau prepares the reader for the profession by pointing out that since religion is a part of life, Emile should be exposed to the various possibilities that will be presented to him as he enters the world. As the goal of Emile's education, according to Rousseau, is to provide him with the ability to judge for himself, he will not lecture to him on religion but provide him with someone who is truly qualified to discuss the matter, the Vicar of Savoy. By way of introducing Emile to the clergyman, Rousseau explains that the vicar was his own mentor and friend, who as a personal favour, told him the story of his faith. After this personal confession, Rousseau explains that "I am weary of speaking in the third person" and resorts to a first person narrative for the remainder of the episode. Von Mücke characterises this change in narrative voice as follows:

> By calling attention to the shift in voice, the text calls attention to its illocutionary dimension and changes its status from a mere story to a personal confession witnessed by the reader. Indeed the manner in which it dramatizes the confession interpolates the reader as confidant and intimate friend, and characterizes the confession as an homage or tribute to the memory of the old vicar. The act of confession is conveyed as a gift …. [in] that it is freely given (*NLH*, 34, 2, 264).

Instead of berating or preaching to the young man, the vicar treats him as an equal, listening to him without disapproval. To illustrate the vicar's character, the narrator recounts an anecdote about the priest, who was so respected and trusted in the town that the locals preferred to give their alms to him rather than the wealthier clergy:

> One day someone had given him money to distribute among the poor, and the young man was mean enough to ask for some of it on the score of poverty. 'No,' he said, 'we are brothers, you belong to me and I must not touch the money entrusted to me'. Then he gave him the sum he had asked for out of his own pocket (*NLH*, 34, 2, 265).

The vicar's profession of faith is, as we would expect, in keeping with his character:

Within the pedagogical context of a wise old priest and young man who had been led astray, who has lost any orientation with regard to religious issues, one would expect some form of religious instruction that would take its cues from the catechism, the codified didactic introduction to, and explication of, doctrinal issues ... By choosing the profession of faith rather than the catechism as the occasion for a dialogue on religion, the formulaic, depersonalised nature of the official religious instruction is avoided; the emphasis is placed on the vicar's belief as filtered by individual experience (*NLH* 34, 2, 258).

In addition to the choice of the personal over the didactic, the vicar chooses a time and place for his confession, sunrise on a hill overlooking a beautiful view of the landscape. The implication is that faith is related to an appreciation of natural beauty, a concept von Mücke describes in cultural terms:

If I relate the 'Profession' to the gradual emergence of aesthetics as an increasingly autonomous domain within the latter half of the eighteenth century, I am thinking of specific concerns of art, such as the nature of imitation, the visual versus the verbal arts, or the nature of our pleasure in tragedy, to give two examples that are typical concerns for eighteenth-century aesthetics (*NLH*, 34, 2, 271).

To conclude, von Mücke demonstrates that the mixture of confession and profession in the episode of the Vicar of Savoy has historical, religious, and literary significance. The emergence of aesthetics in the eighteenth century leads to a view of religion as a form of beauty and of religion as celebrating the beauty of individual piety. Both concepts are based upon love for the individual and for natural beauty. In that sense this interpolated tale, "mise en abyme", or combination of genres can be seen as containing an important element of the education of Emile. Rousseau suggests that rather than didactic lecturing, personal affection and convivial conversation are better pedagogical devices, ones that Rousseau himself adopts with his readers most conspicuously when he shifts from third to first person narrative.

Moving now to a contemporary example of mixed genres that also considers the education of adolescents/young adults, *The Boys*, episode 6, (2019) is a television series about a corporation of corrupt, hypocritical superheroes who are opposed by "The Boys", a group arbitrarily discarded by the company who decide to expose it as corrupt. I choose this episode because it moves from New York, the headquarters of the Vought superhero company, to Sandusky, Ohio, the heartland and mythical source of American superheroes. This geographical relocation or interruption of the narrative, like that of the Vicar of Savoy, involves a move from the moral and physical pollution of the Big Apple to the clean air of the decent if naive country town, a place where the Vicar of Savoy would have felt quite at home. Here the hero Hughie (Jack Quaid) and heroine, Annie (Erin Moriarty) are on a date, chatting affably in the local bar, eventually enjoying their first kiss. Yet they are on opposite sides in this commercial and, as we shall see, mercenary war. Annie is the new superhero while Hughie has joined the opposition because his previous girlfriend, Laura, was accidentally run over by the superhero A-Train (Jesse T. Usher).

The reason this episode opens in Sandusky, Ohio is that Deep (Chace Crawford) has been sent here as punishment after having apologised publicly for sexually abusing Annie. And here we see the genre mixture most starkly, the location of sexual abuse, New York City, and the place of repentance and retreat, Sandusky, Ohio. In this manner we are introduced to the subject of the episode, young, naive innocence versus experienced, powerful, wealthy corruption. This David and Goliath conflict begins with Hughie and

Annie discovering that they have both been deceived and lured into a corrupt corporation that has no interest in anything but profit. Annie finds that the superhero organisation, called Vought, tries to cover up the abuse that she suffered from Deep, the superhero, and then only agrees to a public apology when she threatens to tell her story to the world.

In addition, she discovers that, as Queen Maeve, a more experienced superhero, had warned her, "the house always wins" in that Deep was only able to take advantage of young superheroes because Vought, unwilling to intervene at the time, now lays all the blame on Deep. Since Queen Maeve's autobiography was the source of Annie's desire to be a superhero—as a child she wore out her copy of the book—she realises that her paragon has allowed herself to become merely a public relations facade. In her acceptance that the house always wins and her complicity in the hypocrisy of the company, Queen Maeve appears to Annie a fallen Superwoman who has lost all interest in changing the world for the better.

Meanwhile, in the enemy camp, Hughie is told by Billy Butcher (Karl Urban) that Heartlander (Anthony Starr), the head of Vought, has raped his wife Becca (Shantel VanSenten) who shortly thereafter disappears. Furthermore, Hughie also discovers that Kimiko (Karen Fukuhara), a member of the gang, was rescued when Vought was involved in a military expedition to her native country, somewhere in Asia, where her parents and family were slaughtered. The policy of Vought is to create terrorists abroad so that superheroes will be needed in the military, thereby expanding their business area and influence.

The domestic and personal element, the scene of Hughie and Annie at the bar in Sandusky, is now connected to international terrorism, and Vought, a US company, is directly connected to wars in Asia. The trip to Ohio, involving Annie's relations with Hughie, now has a bearing on terrorism and war in Asia. The purpose of this combination of genres, domestic and international, is to ask whether Annie and Hughie in their endeavours to set right their own lives can have any effect upon the world at large. And by extension, the implication is that an element of the innocence, or perhaps naivety, of Annie and Hughie resides in their assumption that their personal dilemma can be distinguished or resolved separately from that of the world beyond the borders of the United States. The combined genres place Sandusky in the middle, so to speak, a sort of "mise en abyme" or interpolated tale, of national and international terrorism.

This genre mixture has clear historical significance. The modern equivalents of Batman, Spiderman, and Superman are now employees of a large corporation that exploits Superheroes for profit. Any good these individuals achieve is less important—a mere by-product—than the publicity and profit generated by their image. Moreover, like any large firm, this company is hoping for a military contract and thereby becomes an accomplice in foreign wars of terrorism. While Batman, Spiderman or Superman could hope to remedy wrongs in their local environments, be it Gotham or New York City, the new superheroes soon realise that their specific virtuous acts are minimal compared to the damage to the world perpetrated or encouraged by Heartlander's corporation—a dilemma vividly shown in the scene of a superhero cleaning up the beach only to be interrupted by the director who tells everyone to put the rubbish back for a second take. Publicity, image and profit take precedence over any specific acts of decency and helpfulness. By analysis of genre combination, we have returned to the tragic world of Maffesoli, seen in Chapter One. The next section turns to two films for examples of how analysis of genre combination can be an important aid to interpretation not only of literature and television but also of films.

II) Elisabeth Bronfen, "Femme Fatale: Negotiations of Tragic Desire", *NLH*, 35, 1, 103-16 and *Bridget Jones's Baby*, directed by Sharon Maguire, 2017.

Elisabeth Bronfen analyses the film *Double Indemnity* (1944), directed by Billy Wilder, as a combination of femme fatale and film noir. The plot of the movie involves a wife, Phyllis Dietrichson (Barbara Stanwyck), and an insurance salesman, Walter Neff (Fred McMurray), who together murder her husband to collect a double indemnity life insurance policy. From the moment Neff arrives at the house to sell car insurance, Phyllis lures him into her web. Descending the stair with only a towel, Phyllis mesmerises Walter with her anklet, indicating what Bronfen characterises as fetishism, an attraction to a woman as an object. Plotting how to do away with the husband, they dream of life after having completed the deed. Walter obsesses about money, but Phyllis seems more intrigued with the process of luring him into her web.

Bronfen interprets the film in terms of Stanley Cavell's concept of tragedy. In his analysis of *King Lear*, Cavell argues that tragedy is about the consequences of our actions, "consequences that furiously hunt us down ... but we go on doing the things that produced these consequences in the first place". The remedy for this repetition compulsion is not "rebirth or salvation, but the courage or plain prudence to see and to stop" (*NLH*, 35, 1,103).

But Phyllis, the femme fatale, and Walter, the 'noir' character, adopt different attitudes. Like Lady Macbeth, she steels herself to plod through the blood and gore while he, Macbeth-like, frets and worries but is nonetheless impelled forward by fetishistic sexuality and the lure of money. When the crime is finally discovered by the insurance investigator (Edward G. Robinson), Walter blames Phyllis who, all along, has maintained that they are in this together to the bitter end. Finding out that he has turned on her, she comes after him with a gun, wounds him with the first bullet, but, unable to finish the job, is killed by Walter. The conclusion suggests that in spite of being the instigator of the plan, she developed more affection for him than he for her. Walter continued to treat her as an object and was therefore able to do what she was unable to accomplish, namely, murder her with her own pistol.

From a generic point of view what is interesting in this film analysis is that, as Bronfen makes clear, near the end after the killing of Phyllis, Walter becomes the narrator of the film—a change of narrative voice reminiscent of Emile and with similar generic significance—confessing to the investigator and accepting responsibility in spite of his earlier attempt to blame her. Bronfen argues that Phyllis is motivated by a death drive that enables her to take responsibility for the crime, and instead of killing Walter she enjoys his struggle to escape her web. Walter, on the other hand, is only able to admit responsibility after he has murdered his accomplice: he never fully considered her as a person until he confronts her corpse. And his words of confession are very much in the mode of the noir: "'I killed Dietrichson. I killed him for the money and for a woman. I didn't get the money and I didn't get the woman. Pity, isn't it'" (*NLH*, 35,1,107-8). The generic combination of noir and femme fatale serves to emphasise the question of responsibility and how it is a result of seeing the victim as a person, as the other. The femme fatale is, in a sense, another to herself, and therefore comes by guilt and responsibility naturally; the noir has to learn that what he wants is not an object but a subject, that is, money and sex are attached to people who bleed.

This genre combination is clearly appropriate to the historical situation of the film. In 1944, the significance of accepting responsibility was a very timely subject and the manner in which cruelty could be dispensed without immediate guilt or responsibility was of clear historical importance. The Nazis depersonalised their victims so that they became—as was again made manifest many years later in the Eichmann trial—mere numbers, forms of animate detritus. Walter awakens at the end to what many in 1944 saw in the pictures emerging from the death camps, the horrors that result from this frightening psychological process. The belated sense of responsibility of the noir figure and the death wish of the femme fatale places this generic combination in the aftermath of WWII.

Turning now to the present, I consider genre combination in *Bridget Jones's Baby*, 2017, directed by Sharon Maguire. This film combines family romance with passive/aggressive feminism. And although it concludes with the marriage of Bridget and Darcy together with their year-old infant to complete the nuclear family, the final frame of the film shows a newspaper headline announcing that Daniel Cleaver—one of Bridget's old boyfriends—is not dead. Early on in the film, Bridget attends the funeral of Daniel, the arch-rival of Darcy in the previous two Bridget Jones films; at the conclusion, we are left to wonder whether Daniel could once again come into Bridget's life. This family romance is also not without feminist elements: the history of Bridget's sexual relations before marriage is bound up with the previous relationship of Bridget and Darcy that ended unhappily ten years ago. And now with Daniel back who knows what could happen.

In fact, the film begins with Bridget alone on her 43rd birthday, reminding us of similar beginnings for previous Bridget Jones films. On this occasion she has been ditched at the last minute by her gay workout buddy. But this repetition of a familiar opening scene brings with it Bridget's sexual history. Listening to her biological clock telling her to take her ovaries "out of the deep freeze", she resolves to have a fling with the first man she meets at an outdoor concert, clearly a satire on the Glastonbury Festival, a reference made unmistakable by the almost perpetual setting of the festival, sticky mud. Fortunately, she is rescued from the mud by Jack (Patrick Dempsey). After they have "relations", as she puts it, she meets Darcy (Colin Firth), who has just been divorced. They also have "relations", and the question then becomes who is the father of her baby. Although Bridget assures both men that she expects nothing of either of them and can make it alone—a view reinforced by the gynaecologist (Emma Thompson) who explains that she also is a single mother—the baby makes a difference, almost as much to the men as to Bridget and her female friends. For as Bridget points out to her mother, who is running for a Parish Council seat, even middle England is full of single mothers, to say nothing of LGBT members.

Yet even in these contemporary times of gender fluidity, a traditional family for a baby has a high priority. Jack and Darcy compete to look after Bridget even though both are wary of marriage and uncertain about having children. And, in the end, Bridget decides to go ahead with a DNA test to determine the father of her child, believing that she and her child should face the truth. In spite of her flighty lifestyle and occasional lapses, Bridget shows her integrity, especially when confronting her new boss, the slick manager who cares more about audience numbers than news or issues of importance. Upon being sacked, Bridget remarks that she hopes the child in her womb will have more integrity than her new boss.

From a historical perspective, the film is suggesting that family protection is at this time particularly important for a child because the sexual mores in the society at large are so fluid and changeable, highlighted by a female boss who has no compunction about sacking a pregnant woman in her ninth month. But since it is clear that Jack demonstrates that he would be just as good if not a better father than Darcy, the question is why does Bridget choose Darcy. In fact, at the final wedding scene in the church when we see Jack holding the baby we are prepared for him to be the groom. Instead, he is the doting godfather, now a good friend of Darcy's, helping to provide an extended family for the baby.

For Bridget as an independent woman, if not an overt feminist, the decision to marry Darcy not Jack is based upon the past, quite apart from the fact that he, it turns out, is the biological father of her child. When Jack asks if she loves Darcy, she replies that she did once. And in formulating her feelings for Jack, she suggests love is a future possibility. The difference between the two men, in my view, is that Jack, in his benign and caring way, is always advising and directing Bridget. Darcy, no less caring, gives her more independence, and that approach is more suitable to her self-reliant, moderately feminist disposition. The merger of family romance and feminism is a hybrid genre suitable to the personality of Bridget Jones. And again, genre combination provides a key to interpretation: the passive / aggressive feminism of Bridget requires some independence in a family romance that can nurture in her child some of the same feminist freedom that she experienced in her past. The social / historical situation of gender fluidity requires a traditional, as opposed to an "open", marriage, for the security of the child. The next section concerns feminist genre combinations in the forms of translation and private detection.

III) Emily Apter, "Taskography: Translation as a Genre of Literary Labor", *PMLA*, 122, 5, 2007, 1403-13 and *Elementary*, season 5, episode 2, created by Robert Doherty, 2016.

Emily Apter argues that Eleanor Marx's translation of Flaubert's *Madame Bovary* (1873) is itself a genre. The translation in conjunction with the basic bourgeois story of *Madame Bovary* combine to throw new light on the novel. Apter argues that "Marx moved genre theory toward a textual materialism grounded in the labour of translation. She provided, one could say, the terms for a Marxist appropriation of the bourgeois realist novel that departs from orthodox Marxist genre critique" (*PMLA*, 122, 5, 1403).

The traditional Marxist interpretation, according to Apter, sees the novel as the premier bourgeois form that is committed to realism ranging from the inner world of psychology to the outer realm of empirical objects and events. But while Eleanor followed the doctrine of her father, translation took her into a new realm: "In her hands, translation acquires the dispensation of a new Marxist genre theory that crosses art and labor" (*PMLA*, 122, 5, 1405).

Apter suggests that Eleanor Marx laboured over her translation of *Madame Bovary* because she had much in common with the protagonist of the novel. "Eleanor Marx was closer perhaps to Madame Bovary. Vulnerable to depression, she poisoned herself in what looks to have been a copycat suicide inspired by Emma Bovary" (*PMLA*, 1405). Nonetheless, she led anything but a bourgeois life.

Eleanor taught in the London slums, took part in the Second International, churned out articles and broadsides for the Socialist League and the Social Democratic Federation, and proved her mettle as trade unionist and labor organizer ... Eleanor was part of a circle of Victorian women of letters. She was also a feminist who helped introduce Ibsenism into England when she played the role of Nora in a private theatrical and translated a number of Ibsen's plays from the Norwegian (*PMLA*, 1405).

A firm Marxist in her actions and beliefs as well as a devoted follower of her father, Eleanor was well aware that Flaubert did not share her views:

Flaubert was no Marxist. A member of the *rentier* class who prided himself on just how uneconomic his writing was, Flaubert depicts wage labor in *Madame Bovary* only in the personage of Berthe, Madame Bovary's hapless daughter, consigned at the novel's end to factory work … . Compared with Zola, the Goncourt brothers, or early Huysmans each of whom documented the exigencies of wage labor, piecework, domestic work, and sex work in the diverse arenas of the slaughterhouse, the department store, the laundry, the home, and the brothel, Flaubert rates as a pale chronicler (*PMLA*, 1408).

What Eleanor Marx is drawn to in *Madame Bovary*, according to Apter, is the labour of language that is removed from the world of commodity exchange. In *Capital*, Marx speaks of this kind of freedom from the market in general terms.

In fact the realm of freedom actually begins only where labor which is determined by necessity and mundane considerations ceases; thus, in the very nature of things, it lies beyond the sphere of actual material production… . Beyond it [the realm of necessity] begins that development of human energy which is an end in itself, the true realm of freedom (*PMLA*, 1408).

Apter argues that Eleanor, well aware that Flaubert was no Marxist, finds this freedom in the language of *Madame Bovary*. The combination of genres—bourgeois and Marxist— is the result of a gifted translation. Eleanor Marx renders a bourgeois story with descriptive details that suggest intrinsic beauty and craftsmanship beyond any market value. And here we also see the historical/social aspect of this translation; by the time of Eleanor Marx's translation of 1873, some twenty-seven years after the original, the beginnings of the Arts and Crafts Movement, associated with William Morris, were exalting the pride of the craftsman and artist in their work.

In addition to being influenced by her father, Eleanor Marx was surrounded by a new social movement.

Apter argues that, recognising that Flaubert was not a Marxist, Eleanor Marx as a translator became deeply involved with the texture of the language of Flaubert and realised that it contained something different from the bourgeois ideology of the story. For Apter, Marx's translation involves a new way to read *Madame Bovary*:

> To read Flaubert this way is to zoom in on the material origins of his images and on the importance of illustration to his literary techne. In *Madame Bovary*, Flaubert modernized the classical procedures of *ut pictura poesis* ... linking them to modern media and the condition of mechanical reproducibility. His use of caricature, satiric illustrations, maps, portraits, fashion plates, and optical contrivances (spectacles, lorgnons, microscopes) as devices for constructing visual set pieces lent historical density and phantasmagoric surplus value to commodity spectacle (*PMLA*, 1408).

Eleanor's labours over the language and imagery, the literary texture, of the novel highlight descriptive elements that illustrate the pride of the worker in his work quite apart from its price or worth on the market. This effect is not merely verbal but also visual, according to Apter.

> Margaret Cohen's 2004 edition (which, in addition to preserving the revised Marx translation, is heavy on fashion plates) underscores the importance of sartorial templates in Flaubert's realism. The book's illustrations include an Amazon in a riding costume similar to the one that Madame Bovary acquires when she arranges riding excursions with Rodolphe ... Cohen's illustration-

embellished edition prompts further reflection on the labor of literary visualization (*PMLA*, 1409).

This attention to and consideration for the technical aspects of the language and visual imagery may explain why the translation is still used in our time even though Nabokov criticised it severely for what he regarded as an inadequate translation of the imperfect tense. Apter concludes that this Marxist Flaubert is the result of Eleanor's translation, her labour with the specifics, the verbal tesserae of a bourgeois novel.

> One could say that this immaterialized materialism also defines Flaubertian realism, which emerges as a Marxist genre in its obsession with the mystificatory capabilities of objects. This 'Marxist' Flaubert is only underscored by the addition of Eleanor Marx's signature to the novel's English translation. A full reckoning with Eleanor Marx's self-identification as a 'conscientious worker' of translation lends credence to casting translation as a genre of laborious text work effected at the nanoscale of a word-for-word textual world. It also trains a new lens on the well-worn reading of Flaubert as labourer of the 'mot juste' (*PMLA*, 1409).

Apter's notion of "immaterialist materialism" can be seen as a combination of two genres, a materialist story with a background description full of immaterialist details, both visual and textual, that are marked by a vividness and beauty beyond any market value. Apter therefore argues that translation changes the text or our reading of the text, giving new prominence to the immateriality or Marxist ideal more deeply embedded in the bourgeois materialism of the original. As the devoted daughter of Karl Marx, Eleanor—most probably without any conscious wish to exemplify her father's philosophy or the principles of the Arts and Crafts Movement that were current at the time—highlights the immateriality of the language of the bourgeois novel she loves.

> Translation, like generic criticism, effects a subtle generic shift in how we view the literary text. The work becomes something on the order of what I would call *l'œuvre œuvrée*, the worked and working text. No longer a stable object owned by a single author, it emerges as a site of translational or editorial labor (*PMLA*, 1410).

The genre combination of Eleanor Marx's translation highlights new or at least previously neglected elements of *Madame Bovary*. And, most importantly, the translation has stood the test of time, Nabokov notwithstanding, because it continues to speak to the present generation; we still respond to the intrinsic beauty of the details of the bourgeois world of Flaubert's story.

My final example of genre combination in a visual medium is a new translation of Sherlock Holmes stories entitled, *Elementary*, in particular, season 5, episode 2 (2016). This latest Holmes (Jonny Lee Miller) portrays the detective as a reformed drug addict who has been helped to recovery by his female "sober companion", Dr. Joan Watson (Lucy Liu). In this episode, Holmes investigates the death of a friend who died as the result of impure drugs. Following the path of the drug dealer who supplied the fatal dose, Holmes becomes involved with a drug overlord and a corrupt corporation executive. Concerned that one of his suppliers has been murdered, the drug overlord decides to hire Holmes to find out who killed one of his pushers. Holmes agrees to find the killer if the overlord for his part will find out who gave the bad drugs to his friend.

The subplot involves a different genre. While Holmes is enmeshed with the drug underworld, the new version of Watson, Dr. Joan Watson, saves the life of a criminal and aids him in rehabilitation. After serving his time in prison, Shinwell Johnson (Nelson Ellis) starts a new life and asks Watson to help him find his daughter. The two plots function as contrasting genres, the main plot concerning finding the bad guys and the subplot concerned with a good guy, a criminal who is rehabilitated. While Watson is mainly concerned with helping Shinwell, Holmes focuses on catching the criminals but expresses some concern that Watson may be taken in by Shinwell who was, in his criminal past, a member of a violent gang.

The two plots involve two different kinds of risks, Holmes making a deal with a drug overlord and Watson trusting that a convicted criminal is now rehabilitated. The results are not quite what either expected. The man who sold bad drugs is himself murdered and dismembered. Having found his daughter, Shinwell decides to prove himself rehabilitated before resuming contact with her.

Both plots modernise the relationship of Holmes and Watson, the former wildly brilliant but unorthodox and the latter more sober, quietly decent, and kind. And it is important that each has influence upon and input in the plot of the other. The innovation of Watson being a woman makes the partnership a sort of marriage of minds. The double plot serves as a reminder that some criminals are capable of reform if treated with the affectionate intelligence of Dr. Joan Watson, and that Holmes' inspired risk-taking is brilliant if it works but nonetheless very risky. In short, the genre combination, the plot and subplot, suggest two points of view on crime.

I see the double plot as involving two different genres because the ends contrast, one primarily tragic, and the other, comic. This combination presents a new historical perspective on Holmes. A reformed addict, Holmes is brilliant but erratic, taking risks that sometimes produce good results and on other occasions lead to disaster. He therefore needs the sensible, practical Dr. Watson not merely to aid in solving his cases but also to help him maintain his fragile psychological equilibrium. The point of this new version of Sherlock Holmes is that the world has changed since the time of Conan Doyle. The world this present-day Holmes inhabits still has its Moriarty, the eternal enemy, but is also full of criminals who range from those beyond the pale, like the drug lord who dismembers anyone who "disses" him, to those like Shinwell Johnson, who might, if given the opportunity, become productive members of society. After all, this modern Holmes is himself a reformed criminal: the genre combination of tragic and comic indicates that any of us, even Sherlock Holmes himself, could find ourselves on the wrong side of the law. The temptations of our world, particularly given the proliferation of new "designer drugs", are a constant and dangerous lure even for the most respectable among us. Once again, genre combination, as Cohen predicted, is a key to interpretation. And the fact that once again the genre mix involves forms of feminism, a female translator and a Watson who is a woman, speaks to our age: Sherlock Holmes and Karl Marx need to be tempered by a female perspective. Since both the creative and interpretive aspects of genre are involved in history, I turn in the next chapter to how genre alters our conception of history.

Chapter Three

New Literary History and Life: Genre and Artistic Aims

I Peter Hitchcock, "The Genre of Postcoloniality", *NLH*, 34, 2003, 2, 299-330 and *Good Omens*, series one, episode 3, 2019.

II Joseph Farrell, "Classical Genre in Theory and Practice", *NLH*, 34, 3, 383-408 and *Stan and Ollie*, directed by Jon S. Baird, 2018.

III Jonathan L. Crane, "Outsourced Crime Stories: New World Horror, and Genre", *Popular Culture*, 33, 2, 117-36 and *Wallander*, series 4, episode 6, directed by Stephen Apelgren, 2010.

In this chapter I wish to illustrate three elements of Cohen's genre theory that have application to literary history: 1) generic literary history reveals the capacity for radical change, revolutionary notions that question genre itself; 2) generic literary history can expose gradual change, forms of incremental subversion or evolution that are important, if not revolutionary; 3) generic literary history can reveal new and deeper insights that are not apparent to traditional historical methods.

Cohen emphasises that change is intimately bound up with similarity: even the notion of revolution can only be conceived of in relation to that which is being overturned or radically questioned:

> The nature of literary change is thus a study of alterations which can only be understood in terms of the persistence of nonaltered elements of frameworks which provide an identity. Literary change is always connected with or characterized by concepts of knowledge, language, and structure that define some changes as variations of these and others as contradicting, rejecting or overturning them. Change is then a form of adaptation or 'revolution'. But it is the nature of literary structures that change and persistence are present together. The kinds of relations between them account for the kinds of changes critics identify (Rowlett, 280-81).

1) Peter Hitchcock, "The Genre of Postcoloniality", *NLH*, 34, 2, 2003, 299-330 and *Good Omens*, series one, episode 3, 2019.

I begin with postcoloniality because generic change always involves change from coloniality; the result is, or so it would seem, that the postcolonial must therefore be tainted by what it derives from, namely, the colonial genre. Peter Hitchcock grapples with this problem. He begins by asking what would constitute a postcolonial genre: "If postcoloniality were a genre it would be a fascinating paradigm of classification because, like the proletariat among the social classes, its paradoxical mission is to annul its being, the crux of becoming, in the instant of attainment" (*NLH*, 34, 3, 299). Presumably, the object of such a genre would be to subvert its existence, to end coloniality and its means of presentation, postcolonial genres. While Hitchcock recognises that no genre can be said to be totally devoted to postcoloniality, the genre that is most often identified with it is the novel. Certainly, Conrad's *Heart of Darkness* is key in this respect: "And what is historical in Conrad's eloquent indictment of imperialism at work in the Congo has much to say about what is living and dead in the Democratic Republic of the Congo since. The appropriateness of genre is its focus on kinds of narration and the moments of classification" (*NLH*, 34, 2, 300).

Hitchcock sees two forces in the novel often working at odds with one another: the paradox of the postcolonial cannot escape the presence of its other, the colonial:

> When it comes to genre, two histories are implied: the first describes the 'social relation of production' through which genres live and die; the second denotes the conception of genre itself which is subject to the same conditions, yet is discontinuous with the genres it describes. By invoking postcoloniality with these two histories I want to suggest that the political frisson in its project lies not just in mixing genres but also in problematizing the logic of classification which is precisely social in its sedimentations (*NLH*, 34, 2, 300-01).

In specific terms, Conrad skilfully uses the novel to critique colonialism even though the genre that he employs is stained by its bourgeois colonial past. The clash or frisson between these two histories is the focal point of Hitchcock's essay. The conflict between the history of the genre and that of colonialism presents a problem:

> The postcolonial genre exists because it is in the nature of the genre to provide form for the content that challenges what constitutes the genre, and it is in the challenge that

this righteous flexibility is enjoined. But again, what if what proves the integrity of the genre is also what confounds the process that appears at least to provide limitless variation (*NLH*, 34, 2, 303)?

Hitchcock recognises that this problem—the persistent presence within the postcolonial genre of that which it wishes to negate, the colonial genre—is not merely a literary problem but also the dilemma of the political activities of postcolonialism:

> The suppression of genre within postcolonial theory, however, results from the contradictions of postcolonial positioning itself whose general crisis enacts specific elisions. These drawbacks are numerous and are discussed elsewhere as in 'pitfallls,' 'ahistoricism,' or, my favorite, its 'aura,' yet several indicate the severe difficulties that postcoloniality has come to define and that have secondary effects on the question of genre. In broad terms, literary postcolonialism is postcolonialism's most discussed and influential version, so we should not be surprised if this produces a most taciturn or hesitant position regarding the structural politics of the modern state (*NLH*, 34, 2 305).

Hitchcock here makes clear that conflict between the message of postcolonialism and its means of presentation is found not merely in literature but also in the realm of political strategy and action. One reason for this persistent problem is that postcolonialism is about the class system and class is a form of classification or genre, that is, you cannot remove the *class* from *class*ify.

The intensity of categorisation, ordering and classification has political, scientific, cultural, and philosophical correlatives which we might loosely ascribe to modernity, rationalism, empiricism, and the nation. The history of class is, of course, a history of classification and, importantly, the intimate etymological ties between genre and gender shed significant light on the gender wars in the formation of the subject and the category of literature as well. The development of genres as genres traces the political unconscious of modernity: the classificatory ambition in literature is indissoluble from a particular history of self and society (*NLH*, 34, 2, 308).

Not only is class tainted by classification but so too is gender tainted by genre. The stain of the dark past does not, however, wholly prevent light in the future in politics and literature. Hitchcock cites *The Empire Fights Back* as a positive example. "Although their interpretation of what counts for postcolonial has been appropriately questioned, the authors of *The Empire Fights Back* at least raise the issue of rewriting genre as a postcolonial prerogative" (*NLH*, 34, 2, 315). The taint for Hitchcock is a function of language; genre subsumes gender as classification engulfs class; these large categories seem to constrict and prevent change. But those limitations can be overcome. Hitchcock concludes that the problem for postcolonialism lies not in the genre but in the process of "othering" by the critic and political antagonist. Instead of seeing the postcolonial from within the genre of the political establishment, we should see it as pushing, modifying, even bursting out of the old, creating a radically altered envelope, a process enabled by genre.

Why should the example of a complex genre be rooted among the more familiar territory of the genres of Western literature? ... Why endorse the movement from 'comparative simplicity' in Africa to more complex genres in Europe (*NLH*, 34, 2, 323)?

For Hitchcock the postcolonial project will need to use genres but may develop more sophisticated, modified, even radically changed versions of the genres familiar in Western literature. In short, the stain of the colonial past, the taint of its genres, cannot be avoided but may be somewhat modified by generic innovation.

A visual example of this procedure is seen in *Good Omens*, episode three, that first appeared on television in 2019. In Chapter One, I examined episode one of *Good Omens* to suggest that, instead of a religious satire, it is more fruitfully seen as a mock-heroic with the understanding that the mockery or satire is not directed against the heroic, the revered heroes of the bible and of the Judeo-Christian tradition, but of the diminished present-day equivalents who do not measure up to their counterparts of the past. My analysis of episode three—in the generic tradition of the *Beyond the Fringe* sketch about the end-of-the-world cultists analysed in Chapter One—will show how a literal approach to religion often results in farce and in a misunderstanding of the spirit of religion.

This episode involves two sections, a trip through history for Crowley—who has changed his name from Crawley, derived from his early role as the serpent in the Garden of Eden—and Aziraphale, progressing from Noah's ark to the crucifixion at Golgotha, ancient Rome, medieval England, the Globe Theatre in the Elizabethan period, Paris during the Reign of Terror, London during the Blitz of World War II, and 1960s' Soho. The second part of the episode involves the search for Adam Young, believed to be the Antichrist, who has been living the life of an ordinary, decent young boy in Tadfield, Oxfordshire. At the end of the episode Adam uses his "warlock" power to avoid nuclear disaster.

We know from episode one that the two main characters, Aziraphale and Crowley, are anomalies, angels who take human form and live on earth. Moreover, they regard themselves less as angels than as employees of two large corporations—one above and one below—that give them assignments that they both regard as occasionally unnecessary and often wrong and destructive. Nonetheless, the fact that they themselves are religious figures complicates the religious message.

The complexity of the satire is apparent at the scene of Noah's ark. Crowley arrives to see Aziraphale witnessing the loading of Noah's ark. Once he understands that preparations are under way for a flood, Crowley asks what will happen to those left out of the ark. Embarrassed, Aziraphale replies that they will drown. Crowley asks, even the "kids", referring presumably to the young goats but also undoubtedly to the children. When Aziraphale answers that they too will die, Crowley, exclaims, "That sounds like the sort of thing my lot would do." Defending his side, Aziraphale explains, "It is only the locals. God has no problems with the Chinese, the native Americans, or the Australians." Moreover, he continues, "God has produced a rain bow," pronouncing it as two words, something new and foreign to the angel, "and promised there will be no more floods," prompting Crowley to quip, "How kind." The clash or "frisson", to use Hitchcock's term, of genres here—a demon/angel criticizing a biblical story—leads to a different interpretation from that of traditional religious satire.

This scene suggests that the Bible cannot be taken literally, as in "locals" versus the "Chinese", "native Americans or Australians". The butt of the satire is not religion but a literal understanding of Noah's flood: the point left out by the literal rendition of the flood is that those not saved are punished for their lack of spirituality, precisely what is lacking in the literal understanding of the Flood. The friction of genres warns us that, like the appearance of the colonial within the postcolonial, the matter is more complicated than a literal reading will permit. The need for interpretation is emphasised in the next scene at Golgotha when Christ being crucified is moaning in agony. When Aziraphale explains to Crowley that God permitted this painful death to make people be kind to one another, using the same words about kindness that Crowley voiced in the previous scene, the dark angel is understandably sceptical. (We note here the similarity to the Crucifixion in *Life of Brian* analysed in Chapter One. Aziraphale's response to Crowley is as inadequate as the song, "Look on the Bright Side".) The question becomes are a flood and a crucifixion to be understood as God's way of encouraging kindness: since these historical occurrences caused great pain to innocent people we require a more adequate explanation of the events.

Accordingly, the next scene, set in Arthurian England in the fourth century, focuses on the function of religion in history. Here Aziraphale is seeking the black knight, who turns out to be Crowley. Instead of war and bloodshed, the demon-angel suggests that the two make a pact to work together avoiding the war or Armageddon, eliminating much human pain and death. The good angel is at first scandalised but eventually, as is made clear in the next scene, agrees. Here at the Elizabethan Globe Theatre, the two angels flip a coin, one goes to Scotland and the other agrees to perform a minor miracle to fill the playhouse for the performance of *Hamlet*. We may well wonder why a miracle is necessary to fill the playhouse for this great play. Crowley points out that Shakespeare's serious dramas lack the drawing power of the comedies.

The joke here in the middle of this comic episode is on us: we see ourselves indicted, for I cannot imagine anyone watching this programme without laughing uproariously. In short, comedy feeds our deep need for pleasure and laughter, passions that are controlled, even curbed, for the most part, by tragedy, a fact manifest in the next scene, Paris during the reign of terror. Aziraphale is nearly beheaded here, and when he asks Crowley if he is responsible for this massacre, the dark angel points out that it is wholly produced by Man against Man, and uses the human invention of a lethal machine, the guillotine. Secular slaughter with a notable absence of religion produces the type of tragedy seen in *Hamlet*: we recall that Claudius ceases to believe that he can be forgiven by God. The comic/tragic element of this moment in *Good Omens*, reminiscent of the death of Polonius, occurs when the executioner is himself executed after having been miraculously dressed by Crowley in the aristocratic garb previously worn by Aziraphale. Again religious satire is mixed with and complicated by secular irony. And the tragic element of religion is a complex matter that requires interpretation, as does *Hamlet*.

But, as the next scene makes clear, sacred ground is not always secure. (Here we witness a brief interruption that I shall return to later. The two angels meet in a London park. Crowley asks his friend for a poison pill, just in case "things go pear-shaped". Insulted, Aziraphale flounces off.) In the London church during the Blitz, Crowley again saves his angelic counterpart (this time having to hop because he is on consecrated ground) from envoys who have tricked him into bringing them books of "prophecy" for the Führer: we recall that Hitler's form of Armageddon was the Final Solution. Religion in history is subject to the abuse of humans, not merely those who adopt a literal view of the Bible but also those who exploit the spiritual element of mankind for political power. In fact, even Crowley is personally drawn to religion. In the next scene in 1960s' Soho, he has organised a gang to steal holy water from a church. Aziraphale prevents the theft by handing over a thermos of the precious liquid so that Crowley will not have to risk stealing it from the church.

We might well wonder whatever on earth, so to speak, does Crowley want with holy water. Here we need to return to the puzzling scene when Crowley asks Aziraphale for a poison pill. Is the holy water the equivalent of the poison pill? We are reminded of the Roman scene when Aziraphale greets Crowley with a cheerful inquiry about his recent demonic actions. Testily, Crowley replies that there is little else he can do. Is it possible that Crowley wishes to reconvert to his old angelic state or does he just have, shall we say, cold feet? After handing the flask of holy water to Crowley,

Aziraphale proposes that at some time in the future they might have a picnic together or a meal at the Ritz, preparing us for the final episode when they do dine at the Ritz.

The remainder of episode three helps clarify how Armageddon may be avoided. The final section concerns the hunt for the Antichrist child, Adam Young who, we discover, is a seemingly ordinary young boy with extraordinary "warlock" powers. Somehow, we don't know exactly how, he manages to prevent an explosion at a nuclear power plant—the planned beginning of Armageddon—by replacing the nuclear reactor with one of the sweets at his bedside, "a sherbet lemon", all the while remaining asleep—another element of fantasy and sci-fi. The Antichrist starts to seem more like Christ than the Antichrist, much as Crowley moves closer to Aziraphale than to his fellow demons. At the beginning of the episode Crowley chides Aziraphale for giving his light sword to Adam and Eve to guide them in the dark after leaving paradise; now near the end of this episode he accepts the flask of holy water with the reverence of a novitiate priest. The genre of the mock-heroic, which typically combines fantasy and history, as in Noah's flood with those who are left out or as in a sherbet lemon replacing a nuclear reactor, seems now to serve the purpose of religious reconversion or at least a form of re-spiritualisation. Episode Three of *Good Omens* suggests that human spirituality—like the friendship of Crowley and Aziraphale or the love of Adam, the anti-Christ, for his "Dog" and his human parents—is more sustaining and important than the power games played by the religious authorities in Heaven and Hell. If the genre of religious mock-heroic can serve to present an earthly, human form of religion, so the colonial, bourgeois novel can serve the purpose of postcoloniality. In the next section, I turn from radical change or generic innovation to evolution or generic variation.

II) Joseph Farrell, "Classical Genre in Theory and Practice", *NLH*, 34, 3, 383-408 and *Stan and Ollie*, directed Jon S. Baird, 2018.

Cohen describes gradual generic change in the following terms: "Every text distances and even distends the genre to which it belongs. Every text extends, by its contribution, the genre of an ode, elegy, etc., of which it is a part" (Rowlett, 348-9). Since most practical examples of a genre change the genre to some extent, Joseph Farrell examines the relationship between theory and practice in classical literature. He finds that classical theory of genre has had a great deal more impact upon present-day genre theorists than has the practice of classical poets.

> It was once believed that the ancients invented and perfected certain genres and that the works they left might serve as models for later writers. Today belief in ideal patterns is a distant memory, and our interest in genre takes other forms. Classicists, by engaging with specific problems presented by Greek and Roman literature and with the speculative discourse taking place throughout literary studies, have developed very different approaches to genre from the ones that prevailed in the past; but outside of classics, it appears that a traditional (and now outmoded) conception of the role that genre plays in classical literature continues to hold sway. This conception has a distinguished pedigree, and in fact derives from classical genre theory. But the practice of ancient writers was more sophisticated than anything that classical theory could account for, and it is mainly on this practice that classicists now base their understanding of ancient ideas about genre (*NLH*, 3, 34, 383).

Practice, according to Farrell, not only alters the genre but also emboldens other writers to continue to push beyond the boundaries of any laws or rules. By contrast, Farrell explains that classical genre theory is a powerfully essentialising discourse. "First it was widely assumed in antiquity that the kind of poetry that a person wrote was linked to his character. Second, ancient critics further assumed the existence of a similar link between genre and metrical form" (*NLH*, 34, 3, 383). Moreover classical theorists assumed that genres did not permit combinations; they "did not consider the possibility that *The Iliad* might belong to both the epic and the tragic genres, or that it might be useful for some purposes to consider it as an epic and for others to consider it as a tragedy, or the possibility that it could stand partly inside and outside both of these genres, combining elements of each" (*NLH*, 34, 3, 386).

But while practicing poets and dramatists paid lip service to these strict principles, in practice they strayed widely: "despite institutional continuities, the genre of comedy changed so much between the fifth and fourth centuries that the later dramas of Menander and his contemporaries are distinguished from the work of their predecessors by the designation 'New Comedy'. Already in antiquity it was obvious that standard New Comic plots derived from situations that had previously been explored in tragedy, especially by Euripides" (*NLH*, 34, 3, 390).

The Roman poets, according to Farrell, were deeply concerned with genre but the result was very different from the essentialising of classical theorists:

> The Roman poets were indeed concerned, even obsessed with genre as a discursive device, probably as much or more than any other group of poets who ever lived. But their interest in genre as a set of prescriptive rules— which is just about the only way they ever articulate their generic self-awareness—is powerfully undermined,

even to the point of parody, by an attitude of practical inventiveness and what looks like nothing so much as an interest in the untenability of any position founded on the idea of generic essence (*NLH*, 34, 3, 396).

By way of careful historical research and sensitive reading of the literature, Farrell demonstrates that the poets and dramatists understood and probably believed in the rules or laws of genre but their creative works demonstrate an entirely different conception of genre. Farrell concludes:

I hope I have shown that the discourse on genre that is now such an important part of classical studies is far more open than ancient genre theory might have led one to expect. This is so because that discourse is based less on the work of the ancient theoreticians than it is on the vastly more complex and interesting practice of the ancient poets. The most important point I can make in closing is to urge that the implicit theory of genre embedded within Greek and Roman literature comes to play a significant role in any future attempt to assess the history of the discourse about genre (*NLH*, 34, 3, 403).

Farrell's careful study of the writings of classical writers reveals a major disparity between theory and practice even though most writers accepted the theory. Implicit in Farrell's position is the belief that nearly every act of writing within a genre must involve some changes in the genre even on the part of those who believe genres are essential and rule-bound.

The visual example I have chosen for Farrell's genre position is the film, *Stan and Ollie*, 2018. The first point I wish to make is that although the audience within the movie laughs uproariously at Laurel and Hardy performances, the audience at the cinema when I saw it was more subdued, marked by occasional smiles but altogether more sombre. That is because, in my view, an element of tragedy is introduced into this film that focuses on the last years of the comic duo known in their heyday for hilarious comedy with laughter pervading their entire performance even when they were verbally abusing or hitting one another. Nonetheless, the film takes nothing away from the comedy of the pair. Instead, a tragic element is subtly brought in that at times is sad and at others enhances the humour of their skits.

Cohen reminds us that "the choice of genre becomes not a linguistic one but a social one that determines the linguistic one" and he also insists that, like the creator of art, the critic is subject to the same social, cultural and economic forces. "A text can belong to one or more genres, the decision is made by the critic historian…. Such choices always have aims, and these are social, economic, political, and literary" (Rowlett, 306). The social reason for the introduction of tragedy will be discussed shortly, but my own "aim" derives from my social situation in the present-day cinema where it seemed to me the response to Laurel and Hardy had changed from the days when, as the films put it, "they were at the top", a response shown, as previously mentioned, by the audiences depicted in the film itself.

The tragic element of the film involves the failure to secure a film contract for the comic duo even when their performances in theatres in England were sold out. The problem is complex, for it involves the movie moguls and the Hollywood star system of the mid twentieth century. The opening scene with Laurel and Hardy walking through the studio gives us a visual introduction to this vast and expensive industry. Shortly thereafter, we witness a disagreement between Hal Roach, a famous movie mogul, and Stan whose contract has expired, asking for a raise. In a fit of pique, Stan threatens to produce his own films—an empty threat since he does not have the vast amount of capital necessary for such an undertaking—and Roach calls his bluff. Because he is still under contract to Roach, whom he finds intimidating, Ollie agrees to pair up with another comedian. Although the new partnership does not last, Stan feels betrayed, and sixteen years pass before Laurel and Hardy get back together by which time, the mid-1950s, movies have changed in style and Abbott and Costello among others have come to the fore. Moreover, the cost of making a film has skyrocketed so that, not surprisingly, Stan's attempt to find a backer for the film fails.

The result is that Laurel and Hardy carry on doing their act before small live audiences but never again make it into big time Movieland. They are, in short, victims of a Hollywood system that underpaid them in the beginning and then replaced them with younger, less expensive comics, even though in some respects their act improved with age. For the most part, the film follows the Hollywood rejects playing in British provincial towns to scant audiences and earning very little money. Eventually, they catch on in England by dint of sheer persistence and professionalism, but they continue to cling to the forlorn hope of a movie contract. The tour leads to Ollie's heart attack and his eventual retirement that in turn leads to a heated exchange between them about the past when Ollie made a movie with another partner. At this point, their wives mediate between the men who go on to complete the tour before returning to the USA to retire.

The poignancy of their last performance is epitomised by their dance, a routine that is shown repeatedly throughout the film. It is their signature, a routine repeated during the final credits of the film. The dance moves are at once deft and bumbling, a perfectly timed and executed Vaudeville number that is not slick enough for the movies of the 1950s. The comic tragedy is seen most clearly in the conversation during their homeward journey on the deck of the ship. Ollie confesses that he has not told Stan about the failure to raise enough money for the film, but Stan surprises him by saying he already knew. As they sit together holding hands, we feel touched with sadness and admiration for two deeply talented and able comics whose genre has gone out of style or, at least, so it seems from the point of the movie moguls even if we still derive some pleasure from it. So, like the classical theorists, the suits in Hollywood set the rules but in practice we still laugh and cry at what they neglect.

A vivid example of the power of the Hollywood movie moguls of the 1930s and 40s is the recent film *Judy* (2019). While Laurel and Hardy were dominated by Hal Roach Studios, Judy Garland was contracted to MGM as a child star during the period of Stan and Ollie's heyday. One of the most moving scenes in *Judy* occurs when Garland (Renée Zellweger), looking about ten years old, dives into the pool on a movie set against the orders of the director. Towering above the frightened little girl, the head of the studio, probably Samuel Goldwyn, reminds her that she is a little girl from nowhere, owes everything to him, and had better never again interrupt the shooting of his movies. Such is the sort of dominance even adult stars experienced from these authoritarian super-capitalists.

Why now, some fifty years later, are we seeing in films as well as in other media these dominant, not to say tyrannical, movie tycoons exposed? The reasons are various, not the least being the #MeToo movement, the decline of the major Hollywood studios, and the Harvey Weinstein scandal, to name but a few. But even this brief glimpse of these two films in the same genre, what might be called movie-mogul tragedies, suggests how each speaks to the same present-day social phenomenon, the demise of the Hollywood monopoly of movie-making, and yet alters the genre in different ways.

Stan and Ollie suggests the pair could never stand up to Hal Roach because Stan was too aggressive and Ollie too passive; divided, they had no chance against such power. Their mistake was largely a strategic one, a lack of a unified plan. *Judy*, on the other hand, is the sad story of the loss of childhood, a time of fun and joy, taken away from her by Samuel Goldwyn. The bitterness and alcoholism of Judy near the end of her life represents the loss in her own life of the pleasures she so brilliantly portrayed in her most famous film. *The Wizard of Oz*. Both *Judy* and *Stan and Ollie* show how actors and actresses were victimised by studio bosses, one from the point of view of male adults and the other from that of a female child. Each effects the development of the genre in different ways. And, like postcolonial genres, these movie-mogul films, although tainted with the Hollywood studio system, are able to critique that power structure. Moreover, the fact that both of these films are popular shows that the movie moguls, like the ancient classical theorists, were proved wrong in believing these performers were too old and out of style to make new films, let alone ones about their lives as stars of the past. The theoretical authority of classical genre theory, like that of Hollywood studio directors, is called into question by practice and by the theatre of practice, namely, history. At this point, it should be clear that history by means of generic interpretation points to an alternative approach to history, the subject of the next section.

III) Jonathan L. Crane, "Outsourced: Crime Stories, New World Horror, and Genre", *Popular Culture*, 33, 2, 117-36 and *Wallander*, series 4, episode 6, directed by Stephen Apelgren, 2010.

Jonathan Crane demonstrates how "New World" or horror conventions of the United States are infiltrating the genre of crime fiction; the gore usually associated with the horror film has now become commonplace in crime stories:

> Among other media platforms, signal elements from the cinematic splatterfest are infiltrating the prime-time

serial drama, the musical, and high-profile television advertising campaigns. Gory images from lurid horror films notorious for their obscene disregard for human flesh are making particularly disruptive incursions into the enduring genre of crime fiction (Crane, 117).

The result is that recent crime fiction is filled with blood, gore, and violent deaths. The crime genre now is marked by the grotesque forms of violence that are the hallmark of US horror films:

> The articulation of criminal carnage as a hideous pastiche envisioned through reference to American productions allows international writers . . [to] treat the wild work of horrific killers and inventive psychopaths as equivalent to the recent overseas adventures of the United States. In a genre not noted for pointed commentary regarding the direction of foreign policy, this striking correspondence between serial mayhem and American initiatives abroad occasions sharp critiques of U.S. engagements with irregular combatants on other shores (Crane, 119).

Crane maintains that this new element has changed the genre of crime fiction. Nonetheless, some elements of the crime story remain, distinguishing it from the horror movie genre:

> The central inquiry whereby malefactors are run down remains paramount, but the interknit cognitive and sensual apprehension of the terrible sweep of criminal cruelty is radically altered. With the assistance of a foreign register for the depiction of violent mayhem, readers of crime fiction are confronted with criminal deeds that induce the intense revulsion common to the experience of viewing assaultive horror films (Crane, 120).

One of the examples Crane cites is a recent Wallander "Scandi-noir" novel, Henning Mankell's *Faceless Killers*. He describes the murder scene, using a term from the novel, as a "slaughterhouse":

> One of the primary investigators notes in response to a query from a deskbound assistant, 'worse than you could imagine.' Another officer coming up with the only apt comparison on a par with the shocking desecration states that it was like an American movie. It even smelt like blood (Crane, 124).

Near the end of his essay, Crane turns his attention to the cultural effects on the reader of the horror-movie element of crime stories, in particular to Mankell's novel.

> There are several additional observations to be drawn from Mankell's presentation and a reader's likely reception of the crime scene. Despite their common experience of reading a violent procedural, their collective serial engagement, the assembled readers for this work are a varied lot, hailing from vastly different locales. These disparate venues will surely harbor idiosyncratic sets of reading practices that are not wholly identical to the interpretive practices of any other cultural locus. As the Swedish police go about their investigation, an American or Mexican reader will not pick up some of the subtleties or even a gross textual thrust that will be obvious to a marginally literate Dane or thick Finn (Crane, 130).

However, in spite of these important cultural differences in reader response, Crane believes that the violence of the American horror movie genre will break through national and cultural divides:

Yet, despite these signal differences, it is also likely that Mankell's great community of variform readers will share some of the same reading practices. On crucial points of textual import nearly all readers can be trusted to reach similar conclusions ... . When the author and his chorus of cops describe the assault in cinematic detail, a clear vision of the corpse's ragged state and the perilous condition of his throttled mate is shared by a plurality of readers. Furthermore, the collective readership knows just what the inspector means when he refers to the crime scene as an abhorrent display pinched from an American film (Crane, 132).

For Crane, the American horror conventions crossing cultural boundaries have had a general and universal effect: the "filmed American dreadful" has become the "lingua franca" of the crime story genre: "Diverse readers readily grasp exactly how the guilty party has dressed the scene when an American production is indicted. The wet work of a profane killer is horrifically over the top when performed in keeping with a new world shoot" (Crane, 133). Crane concludes his examination of Mankell's works along with those of a number of other successful crime writers as follows:

> By paying explicit homage to the spectacular possibilities of dismemberment and bodily harm achieved by the American horror film, crime fictions may also better execute one of the oldest organizing directives of the genre.... In conjuring up unforgettable scenes of memorable havoc, the evil achievements of cruel men may become more vital and of greater interest than the spadework done by those who labor in the breach. In representations that overturn the status of the good

and true in relation to the unjust, haunting tableaus that depict darkness visible grant benighted outcasts more concentrated attention than they merit (Crane, 135).

Clearly, Crane believes that the increase in crime stories of the depiction of horror raises the stature of criminals and gives more attention to the gore of crime than to those trying to protect us from such crime. Crane's position, in my view, is an example of old literary history because while it employs genre and recognises the mixture of genres, it does not analyse the aims of the writers using these mixtures: nor does he consider the social situation in which this genre combination has occurred and why readers respond positively to this more vivid depiction of crime. I doubt very seriously that Mankell's goal is to glamorise crime or criminals; nor do I believe that he chooses to focus more on the gore of crime than on its solution and prevention.

In the next section, I shall examine a another work by Mankell, that, like *Faceless Killers*, mixes "New World" horror with crime fiction but is shorter and more accessible to a wider audience because of being on television. My purpose is to show that new literary history alters our understanding not only of crime fiction but also of how this genre relates to social and cultural history. The last episode of the Swedish *Wallander* television series involves a young Lithuanian girl, Natalia, who has been smuggled into Sweden by her brother, himself brought in as a labourer on a waste disposal plant. Accidentally, her brother is killed at the plant and his fellow worker is badly injured. The foreman, who is involved in illegal trafficking, tries to cover up the accident by smothering the injured man and disposing of the two bodies in the waste shredder. Seeing him dumping the bodies, Natalia goes into hiding. When found by the Swedish police, she bonds with Wallander's dog Jusi, eventually confessing that she has seen something terrible at the plant. After some harrowing and gory incidents when Natalia is nearly killed, she leads Wallander to the foreman who agrees to testify against the boss of the illegal trafficking operation.

Many elements of American horror movies can be found in this episode. Wallander is injured in one explosion and nearly killed in another. Natalia's brother is seen dying, bleeding profusely from the mouth, and his badly injured fellow worker is smothered to death. Wallander's dog, his constant companion, is so seriously injured by the bomb intended for Wallander that we do not know until the end whether he will survive. And most frightening and horror-movie like is the constant fear on the part of the police and the prosecutor of what this gang may do to the children of the community as well as those of the law enforcement officials.

While employing elements of American horror movie conventions, this episode, like most Wallander episodes, is also distinctly Swedish. The concern for children in general and specifically for Jusi and Natalia is very important. When the dog is injured everyone at the police station is upset, and when the prosecutor's children are threatened, she resigns from the case. In one very moving scene, Wallander brings in the gang leader to ask him whether he sleeps when his children are threatened—-as close as Wallander ever comes to intimidating a suspect. Finally, the episode ends with the prosecutor, clearly someone of romantic interest for Wallander, inviting him to visit her in Stockholm, which, at the time, seems a remote possibility. But when Natalia has been assigned to live with a foster family in Stockholm, Wallander's team members are concerned that the social services might send her on the train alone. Suddenly, Wallander has an idea; he will accompany Natalia to Stockholm and perhaps, we can only speculate, visit the prosecutor. The final scene involves the train ride. A cast on one leg, Jusi sits on Natalia's lap beside Wallander, all together forming a happy if temporary family.

The horror movie genre has been integrated into this crime fiction for the purpose of showing that the abuse of immigrant families threatens Swedish families: protection of immigrant children is seen as intimately tied up with protection of Swedish children. Even the thoroughly hard-nosed woman who hired the illegal immigrant workers will not countenance the foreman's threat to Natalia. The conclusion of this episode that shows how horror-movie conventions combined with this crime drama, a mixture made vivid by Jusi's cast caused by a bomb blast, is to be seen as contributing to a distinctly Swedish social ethic. Violence in the crime genre, like the postcolonialism of the novel, should not be seen as inhering in the genre; the question is always how the genre is used by the creator and received by the audience.

New literary history insists that genre mixing must first be interpreted in literary terms—the aesthetic purpose must be first understood—before applying that analysis to history outside of literature. To return to the metaphor of H. R. Jauss, literature has its own orbit that is surrounded by a series of larger concentric orbits, like planets and moons within a constellation. The interrelation between the various orbits permits each a relative independence although disciplines like history or entire literary periods have a larger, more inclusive orbit. The notion that the incorporation of American horror genre elements in a Swedish crime story leads to aims similar to those in American stories omits literary genre interpretation that alters and refines literary history. The notion that a generic form of violence from one culture has the same function in another culture ignores the aim of the artist and the concrete situation of his culture. The movement of a genre to another culture involves conceptual change. In the next chapter, I consider genre across disciplines to explain Cohen's concept of change.

Chapter Four

Genre Across Disciplines: Conceptual Change

I Dorrit Cohn, "Does Socrates Speak for Plato? Reflections on an Open Question", *NLH*, 32, 3, 2001, 485-500 and *Green Book*, directed by Peter Farrelly, 2018.

II Michael Trattner, "Derrida's Debt to Milton Friedman", *NLH*, 34, 4, 2003, 791-806 and *The Bay*, Episode 6, directed by Robert Quinn, 2019.

III Ann W. Astell and Susannah Brietz Monta, "Genre and the Joining of Literature and Religion: A Question of Kinds", *Religion & Literature*, 46, 2/3, 95-110 and *Lucifer*, series 1, episode 3, produced by Jerry Bruckheimer, 2017.

Cohen describes the conceptual change that has recently taken place in the movement from Modernism to Postmodernism: "In reference to a 'conceptual change', a way of thinking, I do not confine myself to literary study. Unless one assumes that thinking in literature is different in kind from other kinds of verbal thinking (and I do not), conceptual change must refer to all genres" (Rowlett, 307). Later in this lecture, Cohen cites with approval the anthropologist,

Clifford Geertz, for encouraging his colleagues in Anthropology to make use of literary critical procedures:

> Geertz declares that he has taken from the humanities: the need for anthropologists to consider behavior in terms of metaphor (Ricoeur); to consider the interpreter as involved in constructing the interpretation (Fish); to see the act of reading as offering a finishing or completion of the text by the reader (Iser) (Rowlett, 310).

Cohen believes that one of the important reasons for the use of genres across disciplines is to alter ways of thinking or "conceptual change". Describing James Watson's *The Double Helix*, Cohen points out that "joining a personal memoir to the history of the search for genetic change—joining, therefore, an autobiography to a so-called scientific genre—is to use one discourse to undermine another. This genre of scientific history parodies the professional procedure of omitting the actual behaviour of men and women in the scientific community" (Rowlett, 311). Parody, for Cohen, is but one of the generic methods of indicating conceptual change.

I) Dorrit Cohn, "Does Socrates Speak for Plato? Reflections on an Open Question", *NLH*, 32 3, 2001, 485-500.

Dorrit Cohn begins by pointing out that although a number of works have recently appeared questioning whether Socrates always speaks for Plato, the traditional position remains largely unchanged: "the possibility of understanding the dialogues [in literary or dramatic terms] remains largely abstract and theoretical" (*NLH*, 32, 3, 485). Nevertheless, Cohn analyses three of Plato's middle dialogues to expose the problems of equating Socrates with Plato and to resolve an overriding problem in Plato's oeuvre. The "most striking incongruity between what Socrates says and what Plato does occurs near the end of the *Phaedrus* when Socrates attacks writing, the very medium Plato uses to present this position." Most critics ignore this problem, but as one of the few who faces it points out, Socrates' "'criticism of writing is itself written and so itself recanted—by Plato'" (*NLH*, 32, 3, 486). Another example of a disparity, if not contradiction, between Plato and Socrates occurs in the *Republic* when Socrates recommends a mode of narration that avoids the use of dramatic speakers, that is, straightforward authorial narration. But, as we know, Plato throughout most of the *Republic* uses his customary dialogic form.

Finally, Cohn argues that probably the most dramatic of Plato's works, *The Symposium*, is, as its title makes plain, a compendium of many characters beside Socrates, yet most commentators consider only Socrates' position, neglecting the other speakers. Here, Cohn goes beyond merely questioning the authority of Socrates: she proposes instead "the possibility of reading *The Symposium* as a whole against the stream of Socrates' speech," a reading pursued by Martha Nussbaum and Jonathan Lear.

> According to both Nussbaum and Lear ... Plato's sympathies in *The Symposium* lie not with the sober Socrates but with the drunken Alcibiades ... [whose position involves] the knowledge of a deeply human unique, and uniquely valuable experience in love (*NLH*, 32, 3, 489).

Nonetheless, the traditional view of Socrates as Plato's mouthpiece persists because, as Cohn points out, the relationship between philosophy and literature is neglected in both fields, leaving philosophers to pursue the content of Socrates' speeches and the literary critics to consider the significance of their appearance in a dialogic or dramatic form.

In conclusion, Cohn turns to some literary theorists who describe two kinds of dramatic dialogues, the one philosophical and the other literary or dramatic:

> The philosophical dialogue is contextualized in such abstract questions as 'What is justice (the good and true)?' and framed in an atemporal or gnomic present tense: it partakes of arguments ... expressed by disembodied speakers ... aimed at a resolution of the matter at hand. In dramatic and narrative fiction, by contrast, the dialogue is contextualized in such questions as 'What has happened and why?' Or 'What will happen next?' ... and partakes of a time-bound sequence of mimetic events, incarnated in the personalities and existential situations of the characters who are its speakers (*NLH*, 32, 3, 493-94).

Cohn characterises the philosophical dialogue as closed, that is, as excluding any human or historical interest other than the philosophical topic. Literary dialogues, on the other hand, are open to interpretations of the characters and of the context that has a bearing upon their philosophical views. Cohn leaves us with the choice:

> The essential question that presents itself when we take the dialogic form of Plato's work, is whether they lend themselves to be understood as closed or open perspectival structures ... [the former] corresponds to the identification of Plato's views with those of Socrates ... [the latter] makes Socrates into a dramatic character who speaks for himself, not for his author (*NLH*, 32, 3, 496).

Leaving the choice open to the reader, Cohn makes clear that a literary or open reading of some of Plato's dialogues could lead to new philosophical conclusions—that is, to conceptual changes—about Plato's views and/or those of the specific dialogues.

Green Book, directed by Peter Farrelly, 2018

The manner in which generic crossing of disciplines can lead to a change in perception, or in how we think, is vividly represented in *Green Book*. The film concerns the African-American pianist Don Shirley's (Mahershala Ali) travels in 1962 to the mid-west and south of the United States; the film is largely based on a true story. Knowing how controversial and perilous it is for an African-American musician at this time to travel alone, Shirley hires a hefty, fearless driver and bodyguard, Frank "Tony Lip" Lallalonga (Viggo Mortensen). Although Shirley is a well-educated and elegantly mannered classical pianist, Tony, with little formal education, was raised on the streets of the Bronx where people like Don were referred to as "eggplants".

The main focus of the film is on the relationship between these two men, a relationship that in disciplinary terms involves music and psychology. At first, Tony finds Don pretentious and standoffish. But as they encounter difficulties involving discrimination against African-Americans, they each come to the aid of the other and begin, very gradually, to develop respect for one another and finally friendship. Two vivid examples come to mind. One evening Don is arrested in a public bath after being caught naked with another man. Tony immediately sizes up the cops, takes out a large wad of cash, pointing out that Don will be leaving town tomorrow. Why don't the two gentlemen, Tony suggests, take a few hundred dollars and buy themselves a new suit and take their wives out on the town? The policemen accept the handsome bribe, but Don disapproves of being involved in bribery. Tony makes clear that it is preferable to spending time in jail and going to court, Don's first lesson about life on the streets.

However, the tables are turned on Tony when he loses his temper, decks a local law enforcer, and ends up in jail. Don makes a phone call to Robert Kennedy, the Attorney General, and arranges for their release. This element of experience, from the top down, is new and enlightening to Tony. But the beginning of personal rapport between the two comes from music. Tony loves pop music, which is often playing on the radio in the car, much to the annoyance of Don. But as Tony listens to Don playing in concert, he recognises the talent of his boss. And this respect is enhanced when the other members of the trio point out to Tony that Don chose to make this tour, not for the money, but as a means of overcoming prejudice against African-Americans.

The turning point of the film occurs in Birmingham, Alabama, when Don is refused permission to eat in the dining room of the hotel he is due to play in later in the evening. After some disagreement about how to proceed, Tony and Don forfeit their fees, cancel the concert, and go to an African-American "juke joint". Here Don loosens up, joining with the local band to play jazz for the first time in the film. Not surprisingly, Don plays and jives without inhibitions—all at the encouragement of Tony who wants Don to become involved with and use the music of his childhood culture.

As a reward to Tony for becoming more of a partner than a bodyguard, Don drives the last leg of the journey home through a heavy snowstorm so that Tony can keep his promise to his wife to be home at Christmas. Invited to come in, Don arrives later to celebrate Christmas with Tony and his family—probably the first "egg plant" to be invited to the table of Tony, his friends, and family. This friendship across colour lines, probably the first for both of them, results from the interchange between music and psychology. Don sees that Tony respects and enjoys his piano-playing, while Tony understands that this lonely African-American needs to get in touch with his own culture. Tony begins this educational procedure by teaching Don to eat fried chicken with his hands. The interdisciplinary change of perception involves an undermining of racial prejudice, even if only on an individual basis.

Genre analysis features in terms of the journey or odyssey: Don travels to areas of the United States known for extreme prejudice against African-Americans, particularly the Deep South, with the aim of showing that he is as good a professional musician as any white man. By contrast, having just lost his job at the Copacabana and now offered a handsome salary to be a driver and bodyguard, Tony is willing to travel with Don in order to sustain his family. The end results for the two travellers represent, in a sense, the goals of their separate genres. Don's attempt to undermine racial prejudice in the South and mid-west is to little avail but he does make some headway with his driver. Tony, on the other hand, learns with the help of Don—who proofreads and, in some instances rewrites his letters—how to express in writing his love for his wife and family. In fact, Don's tutelage during the trip furthers Tony's bond with his family. This individual crossing of the colour line serves the purpose of family and friendship.

The most important development in the film occurs when the two genres from separate disciplines—music and psychology or street smarts—intermingle. Tony learns from Don how to improve his writing and Don learns from Tony that he has isolated himself from the elements of his past and of his culture that are crucial for his musical career and his quest to combat racial bias. With the encouragement of Tony, Don embraces his own culture, a form of self-love making him capable of love and of being loved. Instead of converting the South, Don changes Tony, who, we should recall, near the beginning of the film, threw out glasses touched by African-American workers given a drink by his wife. I recall an incident in one of my seminars consisting of eight students, seven white men and one African-American woman. In the discussion of tokenism that was very strongly criticised by the white men as a form of hypocrisy, the African-American woman replied, "You have to start somewhere."

The catalyst for this crossing of genre/discipline borders is music, an element of our beings as mysterious as love itself. Interestingly, James Farrelly, the director, tells a story about the music chosen for the film. The Wikipedia entry for *Green Book* informs us that Farrelly, in choosing background music, consulted a singer, Robert Plant, who recommended some songs from the era of the film that are relatively unknown to contemporary audiences, thus avoiding nostalgia while being appropriate for the 1960s when Don Shirley was at the height of his career. Furthermore, at the jazz club near the end of the film, the piece played, Chopin's "Winter Prelude", is not at all characteristic of the Chopin music familiar to most of us. These choices about music—in addition to helping save money on a low budget film—play literally to a deep human responsiveness beyond recognition of the melody, a place deep below the colour line, one of the sources of conceptual change. But crossing disciplines can also call into question conceptual change, as is shown in the next section.

II) Michael Trattner, "Derrida's Debt to Milton Friedman", *NLH*, 34, 4, 2003, 791-806 and *The Bay*, episode 6, directed by Robert Quinn, 2019.

Michael Trattner begins his essay by citing Derrida's remark, in *Given Time: I, Counterfeit Money*, that it is important to analyse the history of money.

Although Derrida focuses on a work by Baudelaire in the mid-19th century, Trattner points out that the change in the history of money mentioned by Derrida did not happen until the late 1960s and 1970s, the time when Derrida's concept of deconstruction was beginning to attract international attention. In fact, Milton Friedman, Trattner points out, described the situation in 1971 as follows:

Until 1971, departures from an international specie standard, at least by major countries, took place infrequently and only at times of crisis. ... [From this point onward] 'irredeemable paper money' is no longer an expedient grasped at in times of crisis; it is the normal state of affairs in countries at peace, facing no domestic crisis, political or economic ... . We are in unexplored terrain (*NLH*, 34, 4, 792).

This "unexplored terrain," Trattner explains, that dematerialises currencies has, for Derrida, a profound effect upon literature: "lifting the 'curse' on irredeemable monies is tantamount to lifting the curse on signs that operate without reference, a central element of Derrida's linguistic project" (*NLH*, 34, 4, 792). The economic change was gradual but continued from the early 1970s to the present. International payments no longer involve money. Payment as such no longer exists; "'payment has become the transfer of debt from one country to another ... .The meaning of economic signs no longer derives from reference to but rather from a code'" (*NLH*, 34, 4, 793).

Trattner therefore argues that Derrida's position in the fields of linguistics, literature, and philosophy is equivalent to Friedman's position in the field of economic theory:

Derrida's argument in *Given Time* comes closest to one of the most important anti-Keynesians, Milton Friedman. Friedman argues that money plays an important role in the economy precisely because it is a system of distributing signifiers which have no referent. He says that money is a social convention that owes its very existence to the mutual acceptance of what from one point of view is a fiction (*NLH*, 34, 4, 793).

Trattner asserts that in this respect Friedman is in agreement with Derrida:

> Sounding very much like a deconstructionist, Friedman goes on to say that money is a 'veil'; what it veils most is its own fictionality. Friedman criticizes previous economic theories for believing that the fictionality of the moment made it irrelevant, that one could always substitute the things exchanged in any discussion of what money was doing. Instead, he argues that changes in the sign system itself, in money, are some of the most important determinants of economic events (*NLH*, 34, 4, 798).

Trattner points out that although Friedman developed his ideas in the 1950s, they did not command general attention until the 1970s when the United States went off the gold standard: "the fictionality of money became an important tenet of all governments and a commonplace of newspaper headlines declaring the latest inflation figures." Trattner therefore asserts that "the economic developments that made inflation a powerful political buzzword contributed to the plausibility of theories such as Derrida's" (*NLH*, 34, 4, 798).

The significance that Trattner attributes to understanding the economic element of deconstruction becomes clear in his analysis of Derrida's challenge to Condillac: Derrida argues that the sign has no relation to production, that is, money has no specific referent outside the realm of language. Trattner places this philosophical issue in history:

> Derrida writes as if what he is doing is simply arguing with Condillac in the ahistorical realm of philosophy, but I suggest rather that he is looking back at the productivity economics of the nineteenth century from the viewpoint

of the consumerist economics of the twentieth, when the theory that production is the central engine of the economic system no longer holds. Derrida finds in theories of signs a parallel to this economic transformation; production is no longer the source of the meaning of signs. Rather, a code produces meaning without distinct acts of production; meanings are then like a stockpile of objects waiting to be used (*NLH*, 34, 4, 802).

Historicizing what Derrida presents as ahistorical or solely philosophical, Trattner leads us to alter our understanding of deconstruction; the subversive nature of Derrida's innovation has been exaggerated. At the same time that Derrida was developing his ideas about deconstruction, economists were accepting and giving long overdue consideration to Friedman's ideas about money having developed from a sign to a code, that is, to the deconstruction of the dollar or pound sterling as a sign for a nation. For Friedman, money has become a free signifier, shifting in the monetary market like words in a language.

> By describing the results of economic transformation he has traced as the end of patriarchy, Derrida's theory implies much more than has happened... . Twentieth-century economics reveals that non-logocentric sign systems can coexist quite well with capitalism and even play a crucial role in the functioning of structures of authority, which apparently can operate quite well without invoking any True Fathers at all (*NLH*, 34, 4, 805).

Trattner thus provides an economic, historical perspective upon deconstruction that transforms what in literary circles was seen as revolutionary into a concept that is compatible with a capitalist, patriarchal establishment. The generic cross-disciplinary move for deconstruction from literary theory/philosophy to economics has produced what Cohen calls a conceptual change, or in this instance, a reassessment of conceptual change, what seemed subversive was really easily accommodated by the establishment. A similar process operates in a recent television series, *The Bay*, episode 6, 2019, the concluding episode of the first series.

DS Lisa Armstrong (Morven Christie) is Family Liaison Officer with The Bay Police Force, located at and clearly representing The Morecambe Bay Police Force in the North of England. The two disciplines that cross in this series involve two views of the family: the genres of personal relations at home and of professional/police family problems. The professional discipline involves Lisa's duty as the appointed FLO in a case involving two missing children. The personal discipline relates to her own two children of similar age to those who, in this case, have gone missing. Since the community is relatively small, the paths of the four children occasionally intersect and we see the crossing of disciplines, that of the professional and the personal. Exemplifying the family genre crossing disciplines, Lisa demonstrates her skills and limitations as a mother and as an FLO, the intermingling of which enables her to solve the case.

The beginning, however, is not auspicious. On a hen night out Lisa has sexual relations with a stranger who, she later learns, is the stepfather of the missing children. When she discovers that this incident has been recorded on a video surveillance camera, she deletes it. Eventually, when this violation of police procedure comes out, she is suspended from active duty, the point at which episode 6 begins. Now with too much spare time on her hands, she begins to make discoveries about her own children who have been looked after by her mother. The parallels between the difficulties of the two families, her own and that of the police case, are clearly the focus of the series.

The family of her police assignment had problems stemming from a neglectful father who became involved with drugs, leaving adolescent children free to pursue drugs and infatuations that they regard as love. At the beginning of episode 6, the suspicions about the stepfather's involvement in drug trafficking are yet to be substantiated, as are the whereabouts of one of the missing children. But as Lisa begins to pay more attention to her own daughter, she learns significant information about her own family and that of the missing children. Specifically, she discovers that the middleman who provides drugs to the local mules is the common thread between the two plots. This smooth operator grooms adolescent girls to do personal favours that do not at first appear to the girls to involve drugs.

Once the girls have become involved and understand that they are delivering drugs, they feel caught or implicated. But, cleverly, Lisa coaxes her daughter Abby (Imogen King) to confess. The scene in which Abby reveals this information to her mother is a good example of generic interdisciplinarity. Having admitted to her own mother that she has been suspended from the police force, Lisa is surprised to be hugged by her and told how proud she is of her daughter for her hard work and dedication as a police woman. In the next scene, Lisa finds Abby with a menacing drug dealer; after rescuing her daughter, Lisa and Abby go to a coffee shop.

This scene shows Lisa's skills as a mother and FLO. With the sort of love her own mother displayed toward her in the previous scene, she regains the confidence of her daughter who confesses her involvement with the drug provider: she now realizes that the middleman duped her into believing that he liked her. With empathy and affection, Lisa gets all the salient—that is, the essential legal—facts from her daughter who finally asks, half-jokingly, "Are you going to arrest me?" With a smile, Lisa replies, "I'm your mum first, an FLO second." Then she tells her daughter that she has been suspended, tearfully admitting that she has let her family down. Abby immediately takes her mother's hand, sincerely assuring her that she is a devoted mother.

This interchange between mother and daughter shows that the two generic disciplines—personal versus professional family—may cross, but the hierarchy remains unchanged: personal family comes first. Paradoxically, Lisa's understanding that such a priority is true for all caring families is what makes her a successful FLO. And it is important that she resolves the case by combining these two skills, always honouring family above professional commitment, a commitment that takes us full circle, from erasing the surveillance tape at the beginning to the end when she apprehends the drug provider and rescues the missing child. The entire case revolves around adolescent infatuation, a topic, as we know from the opening "shagging" scene, that Lisa, a devoted mother with her own sexual needs, understands.

The final scene of this episode makes clear why family empathy is fundamental to a police investigation. Once the stepfather has been found with drugs and the stepdaughter is saved, the police seek to go higher up the food chain to apprehend the drug providers, the big money drug traffickers. The stepfather realises that if he provides this information his life will be in danger because of the likelihood of reprisals from the drug lord. He eventually agrees to reveal their names, but on condition that he speaks only to Lisa who, as we recall, has been suspended. Eventually, a conversation is arranged between the two. Almost immediately, it becomes clear that he insists on Lisa because she alone, he believes, will understand that his family will be vulnerable and that she, unlike the other police officers, can be trusted to make family protection her top priority. After her solemn promise to do her best to look after his family—trusting in her abilities both as a mother and as a FLO—he complies with the police request for the names of the drug lords.

Without Lisa's ability to cross genre disciplines, the major drug sources would have remained at large because the stepfather believes that the protection of his family requires the abilities of both a policewoman and a mother. As Michael Trattner showed how deconstruction seen from an economic perspective is not anti-establishment or subversive, so Lisa shows that the cross-disciplinary family perspective – both personal and public – can change our conception of how a drug dealer can be convinced to turn on his drug lord. She alone, guilty of sexual misconduct and, to some extent, neglect of her children – public and private violations of family values – can inspire trust in the drug dealer. New perspectives often lead to changes of perception. In the next section, cross-disciplinary conceptual change is seen in religious terms.

III) Ann W. Astell and Susannah Brietz Monta, "Genre and the Joining of Literature and Religion: A Question of Kinds", *Religion & Literature*, 46, 2/3, 2014, 95-110 and *Lucifer*, series 1, episode, 3, 2017.

Ann W. Astell and Susannah Brietz Monta believe genre is essential to understanding the relationship between religion and literature:

> Genre study is a critical hinge linking the study of religion and the study of literature, for historical, pedagogical, and theological reasons; we hope to expand upon and develop this observation here. If genre is an intrinsic feature of textuality, a key pedagogical tool for literary instruction, and a continuous presence in the history of literary criticism, and if thinking about genre can make available (if not necessitate or dictate) theological reflections, then to identify ways in which the study of genre might disclose or point towards a theological horizon is to begin to reorient the heart of literary studies (*R and L*, 46, 2/3, 97).

But genre, for Astell and Monta, is not merely the fulfilment of a prescription, fitting a work of art into a pigeon-hole. The traditional notion of prescribed rules is firmly rejected:

> Literary theorists now tend to think of genre not as only, or even primarily, prescriptive (a set of rules or norms to which a work does or does not conform, the work of the critic completed when the task of classification is executed persuasively) but also as cumulative, as a dialogue or dance between an individual work and literary history, a particular piece and its literary forebears. The individual work humbles itself before tradition, perhaps—the bow at the dance's beginning—but tradition too is modified, invited to dance with a new partner (*R and L*, 46, 2/3, 98).

The image of the dance is a poetic version of Cohen's assertion that every instance of a genre affects, alters or radically changes the genre and yet is recognisable as a member of the genre, a form of family resemblance. Astell and Monta believe genre is a conduit for and even shapes our beliefs.

> If genre shapes perception, does it also shape belief? ... As Aristotle knew (albeit perhaps in different ways than those proposed in the *Poetics*), the question of genre is precisely a question of truth (*R and L*, 46, 2/3, 9).

Astell and Monta see genre as intimately bound up with our deepest beliefs that are themselves connected to our concept of truth. To exemplify this position, Astell and Monta turn to *Othello*:

> As an instance of genre shaping belief, knowledge, and experience, we might consider, too, Shakespeare's *Othello*. Up to act 2, Desdemona and Othello may be forgiven for

presuming they are in a comedy: she has been forward in her wooing of her unconventional lover; they have defied a father's marital prohibitions; they have crossed a sea; they have won the approbation of their superiors (the Venetian senate) and secured an important post for the new groom; and they have seen the forbidding father figure chastened. But Iago has a different genre in mind: he persuades Othello that his is not a comic story but a Venetian cuckoldry narrative: 'I know our country disposition well. / In Venice they do let heaven see the pranks / They dare not show their husbands' (3.3.206-8). According to Iago's narrative Desdemona will behave as a young fabliau wife always does: adulterously (*R and L*, 46, 2/3, 102).

By applying a religious viewpoint to a literary genre, Astell and Monta offer an innovative interpretation of *Othello*: it is not only a tragedy of jealousy but also one about the genre of the portrayal of women as synonymous with Original Sin. Iago manages to convince Othello that not only is Desdemona unfaithful but that her behaviour is no surprise since she is precisely the type of young woman we are familiar with in the genre of the fabliau, a genre according to Iago, well-known in Venice. Monta and Astell argue that our beliefs are shaped by stories as our stories are shaped by our beliefs. Certainly, one of the great puzzles of *Othello* is how could the Moor believe that someone as pure and deeply loving as Desdemona would be capable of adultery. Here the suggestion is that, in addition to the handkerchief, Iago employs a literary argument; surely, such seemingly pure young beautiful women are the stock characters of the fabliau. Although Iago does not mention the fabliau, Astell and Monta suggest that the implicit reference is there, an allusion to a genre commonly known at the time of the play.

Aside from whether or not we agree that genres are intimately bound up with religious belief and truth. Monta and Astell have suggested how interdisciplinary genre analysis—namely religion and literature—produces a change in perception. Othello's jealousy is encouraged by a stereotypical image of women. Iago can make use of this view of women because fabliaux of the day were popular so that this choice of genre is historically appropriate to the Venetian society of the day. Whether we characterise the change in perception as religious, like Monta and Astell, or secular is less important to my argument than that it results from using genre to cross disciplines. I suspect Cohen would argue that all sorts of beliefs are involved in genre, including those of religion.

Lucifer, series one, episode, 3, 2017.

If Astell and Monta take a religious viewpoint above the mortal fray of language, Lucifer (Tom Ellis) sees it from below. A disillusioned devil who has left hell, he defies his "Dad", better known as God, and takes a vacation to Los Angeles where he pairs up with a single mother LAPD detective, Chloe Decker (Lauren German). When asked by his psychiatrist Dr. Linda Martin (Rachel Harris) why he chose LA, he mentions the weather and Mexican food, but she points out that most people come to LA to "reinvent themselves", and that, as we shall see, is the motif of this episode.

The partnership here is between these two opposite personality types, the commonsensical, factually grounded LAPD detective and the wild, spiritually perverse, instinctive devil, who for our purposes represent the two very different disciplines, forensic science versus a strange kind of extra-sensory psychological perception. While Decker is a clever cop focusing on the facts, Lucifer uses his ability to tempt all mortals, or as he puts it, staring at his victim with red eyes, "tell me about your deepest desires". The problem in solving many police cases is that often the facts alone are insufficient or misleading. At the same time, insights into the inner soul can also be misleading or lack sufficient proof from a legal perspective. Gradually, the pair accept that each is a check upon the other, and that when the two reinforce one another, they probably have solved the crime.

The episode begins with Lucifer encouraging a young "virgin" football star to lose his virginity with his date. After they have spent a night together, the football star awakens to find his sexual partner dead in the swimming pool. On the woman's cell phone is a video of the football player discovering that the sex scene between them is being recorded. So Decker regards him as the main suspect, but Lucifer can see that he is not capable of murder. Eventually, they work out that the person who has a motive and no alibi is also capable of murder.

In order to get a confession from the murderer, Decker and Lucifer resort to a woman—a sort of Hollywood facilitator—who helps solve the crime but also informs Lucifer that there is an impostor, a false Lucifer, who is ruining his reputation. Lucifer arranges for the impostor to be delivered to his club, where he threatens to torture and ruin him for life. But having looked into the soul of this pathetic counterfeit devil and recalling his shrink's suggestion that he may overreact to this harmless form of identity theft, Lucifer lets him go without punishment. His associates from Hell believe that he is going soft, becoming more human. Indeed, he is intrigued by the fact that Decker is the only woman, including his own psychiatrist, who does not succumb to his charms. By contrast, Decker, who throughout the episode has been sceptical about Lucifer's spiritual abilities, is reviewing videos of his acts during the case that defy empirical explanation.

The conclusion shows both Decker and Lucifer maintaining their difference but edging closer to one another not only because each is attracted to the other, but also because they share a goal, the desire to protect the innocent and punish the guilty. Achieving this aim together suggests not only a personal relationship between them but also an interdisciplinary approach to crime, a devotion to the facts and an attempt to size up the inner beings of the suspects. If the motif of this episode is reinvention of the self, Decker and Lucifer are equally involved in this process. Loth to admit how much he helped solve the crime, she is clearly intrigued and puzzled by his behaviour as he is fascinated by her ability to resist his charms.

When Lucifer is severely criticized for becoming soft and semi-human, he overtly scoffs at the devils' accusations but confesses to his psychiatrist, that he is enjoying the change. Interdisciplinarity not only helps resolve problems that each discipline on its own could not but also modifies the disciplines themselves. Genres cross borders and change borders. The conceptual changes here involve not only Decker and Lucifer, who never expected to be attracted by one another, but also the genre of the police procedural. "Just the facts", the motto of many examples of this genre, *Lucifer* suggests, needs to be supplemented with making proper use of the facts requiring some instinctive insight into people. The fact-bound genre of the police procedural can be penetrated by a devil figure that breaks all the rules but is occasionally brilliant and useful. Most interlopers into established disciplines offering new conceptions are seen as demons of a sort. But sometimes they provide us with useful conceptual changes. The question for the next chapter is change from what, since change in itself is only understood in relation to repetition or sameness: change, like genre, requires constancy against which to measure change.

Chapter Five

Genre and Change: Change from What?

I Micah Mattix, "Periodization and Difference", *NLH*, 35, 4, 2004, 685-97 and *Bohemian Rhapsody*, directed by Brian Singer, 2018.

II Thomas Pavel, "Literary Genres as Norms and Good Habits", *NLH*, 34, 2003, 2, 201-210 and *Rocketman*, directed by Dexter Fletcher and written by Lee Hall, 2019.

III Lois Parkinson Zamora, "Eccentric Periodization: Comparative Perspectives on the Enlightenment and the Baroque", *PMLA*, 128, 3, 2013, 690-697 and *Once Upon a Time in Hollywood*, directed by Quentin Tarantino, 2019.

Not merely the subject of the historian, change is central to all disciplines and to knowledge itself. Because we are immersed in the stream of time, change is our means of distinguishing one object or action from another. Even in the earliest oral cultures, genre was the means used for this purpose even though genre is itself subject to change. Cohen explains this fundamental notion as follows:

Genre ... in old (oral) organized societies ... served to distinguish one kind of communication from another... From these early beginnings between poet and audience we note that genres possessed social purposes in a community and that genres arose to contrast, complement, define each other's aims (Rowlett, 88).

As a starting point in studying change, Cohen proposes the distinction between variation and innovation, that is, between incremental change and radical change, the former being less overt than the latter. But preceding the analysis of change of individual works, we need to understand larger segments of change or history, namely, eras and periods. Cohen explains:

Perhaps the most elementary distinction is one that must precede interpretation of individual works ... the recognition that history must be segmented to be comprehensible. Such segments are not arbitrary divisions, but presuppose some rationale such as importance or consequentiality, some natural divisions (infancy, childhood, etc.) or some common stylistic features that can account for the kind and sequence of changes ... The beginning of a change I call 'innovation,' its continuity, development and extension I identify as 'variation' (Rowlett, 189-90).

Cohen explains that innovation is often identified by an alteration in form: "innovation is marked by the attempt to alter the poetic techniques characteristic of a form ... . To put the issue in the language of problem solving, the poet finds the problems posed in the form need reordering" (Rowlett, 200). Moreover, generic change involves not only innovation of individual works but also of the generic hierarchy or system of interrelations: "innovation cannot be understood by application to a single literary form ... because forms themselves are interrelated in dealing with the varied possibilities of experience in poetry" (Rowlett, 217).

Innovation and variation, for Cohen, are key to understanding and articulating the distinctions between literary periods, the segments of change found in all disciplines. Always involving the interrelation of forms, innovation and variation involve not only a literary or formal concern but also a social one:

> [This hypothesis] suggests interrelation of forms is not arrived at by part-whole relationships within a poem, but by how forms function as a group in society. Statements about the interrelations of form, about the relations of form to nonliterary experience, deal with analysis of classificatory systems. The understanding of such systems becomes the precondition for interpretation; it is not determined by interpretation of specific poems (Rowlett, 218).

Since social analysis is a necessary basis of interpretation, Cohen argues that "the historical study of literature is a necessary condition for any literary analysis" (Rowlett, 221). In particular, the literary interpreter must understand the social norms of a literary period:

> The concept of period norm ... [applies to] works over a considerable period of time . . .[that] reveal analogues or similar implications of construction. These implications can be seen retrospectively in the kinds of genres that are most practiced—as the georgic, satire, and epistle in the eighteenth century or the variety of lyric in the period immediately following ... The interpreter's recognition of a generic hierarchy is necessary to explain why satiric

and georgic poems, for example, became comprehensive forms that can include features from most other types not previously associated with them (Rowlett, 231).

The analysis of generic hierarchies also involves an understanding of how social norms are related to the political situation of the period: "a period norm must take account of the different political implications of literary works at any one time." Moreover, a period norm may also take on psychological implications; "the distinction between the nonconscious norm of the writer and his subject matter serves to explain why works that support Walpole and those that attack him can, nonetheless, be part of the same norm" (Rowlett, 231). I turn in this first section to the problem of periodisation.

I) Micah Mattix, "Periodization and Difference", *NLH*, 35, 4, 685-97, 2004 and *Bohemian Rhapsody*, directed by Brian Singer, 2018.

Micah Mattix argues that the literary periods used now are inadequate, particularly in recognising difference, or what Cohen calls innovation. Mattix begins by explaining that periodisation is itself relatively recent, dating from the late eighteenth century, and that it has been criticised regularly since then. Most recently, "Robert Rehder has shown how the use of period terms is, in many ways ahistorical, as authors who do not exhibit the stylistic elements of the supposed period in which they live are treated as somehow outside their own time." The response to such critiques is that the function of the period designation is to highlight difference and originality. But Mattix counters that in practice the opposite occurs: "far from helping to delineate how a particular author is different, period terms obscure it by superimposing a predetermined schema that is reductive (*NLH*, 35, 4, 685).

As an example of how difference is neglected and obscured Mattix turns to the poetry of Frank O'Hara. Even a careful critic like David Perkins, who recognised the distinctive nature of O'Hara's poetry, does not do it justice: "while Perkins is sensitive enough to notice that the styles of Ginsberg's and O'Hara's poetry as well as those of Olson's and Lowell's are in fact quite different, he is ultimately unable to examine those differences in any detail because of a previous commitment to the notion of a period style" (*NLH*, 35, 4, 689).

In fact, O'Hara himself recognised that his poetry was different from most of that of his period because he was influenced by poets of earlier periods, from Wallace Stevens to William Wordsworth. Although one critic does notice the similarity as well as the differences between the styles of O'Hara and Stevens, the period distinction prevents further discussion: "yet both these differences and similarities go undetected when the two poets are separated by the two categories of periods". Mattix continues: "Style in poetry does not necessarily develop in periods ... . But how a poet differs from contemporary poets in the same period or how he is similar to poets in previous periods, is rarely, if ever mentioned" (*NLH*, 35, 5, 692).

Some literary histories, according to Mattix, attempt to account for difference by making subdivisions within periods.

> Helen Vendler's proposal is that the solution to reductive periods is more categorization ... These further divisions, however, have not corrected the reductive nature of period terms, but accentuated it. In Halberg's chapter on the avant-garde in American poetry ... [the] added divisions fail to make the heterogeneous nature of American poetry apparent, but ... have displaced the subject of poetry almost entirely in favor of discussion of such things as 'Black Mountain avant-gardes,' 'New York

avant-gardes,' 'the Black Arts Movement,' and so forth … . Period differences do not make difference apparent, and, in practice, are used for convenience (*NLH*, 35. 4. 694).

In conclusion, Mattix agrees that period divisions serve a purpose but that the present ones are counter-productive. He welcomes Cohen's suggestion of an alternative:

> Ralph Cohen argues that change and development ought to be analyzed in terms of their genre over a period of time, the duration of which is, in turn, determined by identifiable changes in the texts belonging to that particular genre (*NLH*, 35,4, 695).

Cohen's point here is that distinct genres within a period develop at different rates and relate to the norms of the period in different ways. In an essay published posthumously in *New Literary History*, edited by John L. Rowlett, Cohen reiterated his position that genre mixtures combined with social norms are the key to understanding and creating periods that are useful. Summarising his analysis of the Augustan period, Cohen points to the significance of genre and historical norms:

> The didactic forms [of the Augustan period] arose in a period of civil dissension and war, and the function of the mixtures was to address a diverse audience and to persuade them to avoid violence and factionalism. The changing view of the audience was noted by Addison, who urged upon his readers the value of the 'spectatorial' role (*NLH*, 50, 1, 125).

We notice here that the first sentence above refers to the social situation and that the final sentence is an allusion to literature,

Addison's *The Spectator*; both considerations are needed to understand genres, norms, and periods. Cohen concludes this essay with a reminder to those who would like to avoid the burden of defining literary periods that "since systems of forms govern a period, any interpretation of a form within it depends upon a period hypothesis as its context" (*NLH*, 50, 1, 126). We cannot as interpreters of individual works of art avoid the problem of periodisation. Without larger categories, such as genres, norms, and periods, we cannot differentiate the individual work of art, event, or thought because change can only be understood as change from what, a principle exemplified in *Bohemian Rhapsody*.

Clearly genre, and social and political norms, as well as musical periods are central concerns here. The title *Bohemian Rhapsody* refers to a song that is rejected by the producer because it is too long and combines opera and rock; not only is it too long for the radio disc jockeys who want three-minute segments but it also combines a highly popular genre, rock, with one that, according to the producer, nobody likes because from a now dated period, opera. It therefore exemplifies Mattix's point that anomalous works that do not fit current categories or periods are ignored, neglected, or never see the light of day.

But Queen proves the producer wrong; at the end of the film, the audience at Wembley Stadium sings "Bohemian Rhapsody" along with Queen. In fact, as Freddie Mercury (Rani Malek) had predicted, the innovative genre combination—opera and pop—of "Bohemian Rhapsody" helped give Queen its distinctive name recognition. The group is introduced at the Live Aid concert as "Her Majesty, the Queen", with one of the key songs played being "Bohemian Rhapsody". The rock genre has successfully incorporated opera into a song that reached the top of the hit parade. Moreover, the genre hierarchy that would ordinarily place opera well above rock, as well as the period that sees it as dated, has been reversed in that the latter subsumes the former. The rise of rock performers above opera singers—certainly in terms of earnings if not social prestige—is one of the distinctive social norms of this time period. Moreover, the resurgence of opera, at least in this particular song, further complicates the period norm.

The final concert of the film, the Live Aid performance, reveals the socio-political significance of Queen and particularly of Freddie Mercury: the norms are both transgressed and confirmed. Freddie's spurned lover Paul (Allen Leech) declares on television that the pop star takes a new homosexual lover every night. Although only the band members know that Freddie has AIDS, Paul's revelations place Freddie among those marginalised homosexuals of the 1970s and 80s whom we see throughout the film dying of AIDS in hospitals alone, without their families. Here we see the significance of periods or historical eras.

The music of Queen speaks to and of these people, no less marginalised than those starving in Africa. But Freddie does not violate all social and political norms. After having left the group to go off on his own, Freddie now appeals to his ex-band members to come together again as a family. In addition, after a long absence Freddie visits his biological family, at which point his father for the first time watches his concert with the realisation that this Live Aid concert represents the values of family and charity that he has sought to inculcate in his son.

However, Freddie is much more successful at transgressing the genres of music than the social norms or categories of sexuality in his life. In fact, as he points out to the band, he is a performer who gives the audience what they want, along with—omitted in his self-description—what he loves and wishes to express in music. Ironically, his stage performance involves many sexual roles, including at one point singing in drag. But what is acceptable on stage is not necessarily permitted off stage: in particular during the 1970s and 80s when homosexuality was beginning to be accepted or at least recognised by way of AIDS awareness, bisexuality was not. So Freddie moves from heterosexuality—love of and marriage to Mary—to homosexuality in his relationship with Paul and later Jim. At the end of the film, we are left to wonder if Freddy is really bisexual, since he maintains that he still loves Mary even after she remarries and is pregnant, while he remains involved with Jim.

Clearly, the relationship between socio-political norms, genres, and periods is complex, seldom straightforward. For the past few generations, the pop music scene has been ahead of the society of the audience in terms of sexual mores; performers like Freddie Mercury and Elton John—it is not coincidental that they shared a manager— were able to get away with flaunting their homosexuality on stage because they were great singers and musicians and their performance was bound up with sexual role-playing. Great performers are allowed to push the socio-political norms, but only within certain limits, as is seen in the film during the press conference when the band is subjected to embarrassing personal questions, particularly when Freddie is asked if his father approves of his lifestyle.

Although interrelated, norms, genres, and periods develop at different paces. Probably, Freddie—although possibly bisexual— along with Elton John helped revise the sexual norm toward acceptance of homosexuality. This influence upon the social norms is also aided by the genre hierarchy change; perhaps the inclusion of opera lends an aura of respectability to Freddie. The term "rhapsody" in the title song furthers that end, adding a bit of class or the classical to "Bohemian Rhapsody". The complex relationship between genres and social norms is further clarified in the next section. At this point we have seen how interpretation of the film is based upon a period concept, itself based upon genre mixtures and social and historical norms. A study of change—and interpretation must involve change—needs these three larger categories to define the "what" of "change from what". The next section further considers the relationship between genres and social norms.

II) Thomas Pavel, "Literary Genres as Norms and Good Habits", *NLH*, 34, 2, 201-10 and *Rocketman*, 2019.

Thomas Pavel considers the relationship between genres and norms. He begins by pointing to two extreme positions on genre which are for him false temptations: "Those who think about literary (and cultural) genres are ... subject to two temptations: one is to freeze generic features, reducing them to immutable formulas, the other is to deny genres any conceptual stability" (*NLH*, 34, 2 201). Pavel believes that there is a middle ground between these two extremes. Genres are flexible, changing with each instance of use as well as in history and yet they maintain enough stability to be of use in interpretation. The evolution of genres does not completely obscure the trace of that from which they evolved.

> Genre is a crucial interpretive tool because it is a crucial artistic tool in the first place. Literary texts are neither natural phenomena subject to scientific dissection, nor miracles performed by gods and thus worthy of worship, but fruits of human talent and labor. To understand them we need to appreciate the efforts that went into their production. Genre helps us figure out the nature of a literary work because the person who wrote it and the culture for which that person labored used genre as guideline for literary creation (*NLH*, 34, 2, 202).

Having established that genres are malleable enough to permit individual expression and subject to historical development, Pavel considers whether genres are norms, which he defines as social conventions or good habits, ranging from everyday greetings to more complex matters like the appropriateness of the terms "tragic" and "comic". Pavel asserts that formal genres clearly are norms—as the sonnet must have fourteen lines—and that the more complex genres are to be understood as categories:

> These categories have a normative content simply in the sense that in the traditions in which they strive, certain customs of literary production prevail. Writers, who like most human beings, know their own interest tend to follow these customs or habits. But does this mean that the genres of tragedy, comedy, and so forth have an internal set of normative requirements independent from social custom? My answer is affirmative (*NLH*, 34, 2, 205-6).

Pavel concludes that seeing genres as norms or good habits clarifies the puzzling quality of genres; together norms and genres are part of the routine followed by professionals in the field, like a surgeon putting on sterile gloves. Genres are for Pavel marked by conventional, routine procedures.

> To see genre as a set of good recipes or good habits of the trade oriented toward the achievement of definite artistic goals makes the instability of generic categories less puzzling and less threatening. Genres other than strictly formal ones are unstable and flexible because the goals pursued by writers with their help vary, as do the way of achieving these goals. The good habits the writers form in the process (the recipes they discover or, if you want, the norms they create) are therefore subject to change (*NLH*, 34, 2, 210).

To assess this idea of the relation of norms and genres I shall examine *Rocketman*, 2019. The early and middle years of the life of Elton John (Taron Egerton) are told as a musical, a genre with reference to distinct social norms. In fact, the opening scene makes clear that the film is autobiographical in that Elton John is presenting himself to a psychological therapy group session. Since the conclusion of the film returns to the sanatorium where presumably the first scene was located, we can surmise that the entire film is Elton John's musical rendition of his life up to that point, presumably 1972, when the song *Rocketman* was first performed.

By way of the scenes from Elton's childhood, we come to understand that he suffers from a lack of self-love stemming from his early childhood of neglect by his mother and a forlorn hope that his father would hug him. Even near the end of the film when Elton, now an international success, visits his father—who divorced his mother, remarried and has two sons with his second wife—they remain at a distance without anything like a hug. In fact, his father refuses Elton's offer of free tickets to his concert, and when for a brief moment Elton is pleased that one of his albums is produced for his autograph, he is brought down hard by his father explaining that the dedication is not for himself but for a friend who, as he indelicately puts it, "is a fan".

Elton's mother is equally cold and unloving. Her response to his tortured phone call admitting that he is a homosexual, is deeply disappointing: in her characteristic offhand manner, she claims having always known he was gay, adding salt to the wound by pointing out that he must expect never to be loved. This parental response helps us understand why Elton's manager John Reid (Richard Madden), insists that Elton tell his family about his homosexuality so that they do not reveal anything to the press. Clearly, during this period of the 1960s the sexual stigma of homosexuality would be detrimental to Elton's career.

We are, however, left in doubt as to what to make of this presentation of Elton's life with his family since at one point before the divorce his parents suddenly enter into the musical and sing. Their performance itself is quite out of character; equally inconsistent with their personae are the lyrics that they voice. These admissions of their inner being—the mother's need for and the father's inability to feel love—leave us to wonder if this autobiographical account is factual or fanciful. This scene presents the question of the relationship between the world of music and that outside of it, reality, bringing us to the problem that Pavel raises between norms and genres.

Seeing and hearing these repressed parents burst into song, we recognise the conventions of the genre of musical comedy where emotional expression in song is expected and acceptable. But this form of self-expression clashes with the social norms of the real or autobiographical world that Elton presumably endured; in that world the last thing his parents would do is reveal in his presence any personal feelings about love. Indeed, this contradiction between no expression of parental love in his childhood and the emotional fullness of his music is the subject of *Rocketman*. Moreover, the procedure of the film is to reveal the difficult, lonely road that Elton travelled before being outed as a homosexual, and, even more difficult, his acceptance of himself as a homosexual—represented by the climactic scene when he hugs the little boy of his childhood.

That key moment of Elton embracing his past with the addition of love, not only for himself but even in an attempt to forgive his parents, is the final stage leading to a new life beyond drink, drugs and other excess—except apparently for shopping. This embrace by Elton the adult of Elton the child is based upon difference as well as similarity. Both are Elton, although separated by many years: each inhabits a different genre with the different social norms of distinct historical eras. The film shows that the borders between these two genres can be bridged to some extent by psychology— Elton's journey—and by historical development, as we saw in the previous section when in the 1980s and 90s homosexuality ceased to have the stigma prevalent in Elton's youth and middle years.

But the connection between stage and life in the film involves a harrowing journey of loneliness, physical and psychological pain, and self-doubt. At the same time the film also shows that the bridge of anguish for Elton is for us the basis of his heroic performance showing all his talent for music and outlandish self-presentation. The magnificent scenes of the film and of Elton's life up to this point constitute our pleasure and his pain. And the difference helps us understand that what we love and enjoy in Elton's performance is the source of his anguish and ultimately of his triumph. Triumph requires obstacles, difference.

But the point to be emphasised for the purpose of genre theory is that artistic genres and generic conventions, while related to sexual and psychological norms of society are different and often proceed at a different pace. Characteristically Cohen made this clear in one sentence of his introductory remarks about Pavel's essay:

> The assumption that writers are governed only by artistic considerations in their writings seems to disregard the social as well as personal features in the construction of genres (*NLH*, 34, 2, viii).

Social norms and generic conventions affect one another, but life and art remain different.

The genre hierarchy here is also important. *Rocketman* incorporates the song of the title within the autobiography of Elton, suggesting that his life on stage, as represented by the song, is not sufficient to satisfy his need for love, his desire for happiness. He wants and needs to find a pathway from the stage to life and this move requires a change in the genre hierarchy. At the same time, the fact that Elton offers his autobiography as a musical performance makes clear that he wants to be able to live a life off stage like that of, or at least as sexually liberated as, that on stage.

We are told in print at the end of the film that for the past 28 years he has lived free of alcohol and drugs with the same partner.

That does not sound to me like the life we have seen on stage in *Rocketman*. This printed announcement at the end of the film is insisting on the difference between the social norms during the time of the film and those operative now. And it could be argued that since 2019 when *Rocketman* premiered, homosexuality has become more acceptable than at the time depicted in the film. Now Elton can compromise history for the purpose of the genre conventions of the musical: alongside their gay son, his parents can sing of their own desperate searches for love, something they would not have contemplated doing at the time. Is this clash between social norms and generic conventions introduced for the purpose of making the film "with it" and up-to-date or to announce a change in social norms, or possibly both?

Social norms differ from generic conventions in that they both affect and are affected by history but develop and change in different ways: the generic conventions of the musical do not permit repression of the expression of the need for love that social norms may require. Musicals require the expression of emotion. The next question that arises from the distinction between social norms and generic conventions is whether the categories of history or periods can do justice to both.

III) Lois Parkinson Zamora, "Eccentric Periodization: Comparative Perspectives on the Enlightenment and the Baroque", *PMLA*, 128, 3, May 2013, 690-697 and *Once Upon a Time in Hollywood*, directed by Quentin Tarantino, 2019.

Lois Parkinson Zamora begins with the problem of applying large cultural period concepts, like the Enlightenment and the Baroque, to a small or more local region, in this instance, Mexico:

Cultural historians regularly refer to the late eighteenth and early nineteenth Century in Mexico as 'la illustración' and the intellectuals of the time as 'los illusos', 'illuminated ones', but this did not stop the Mexican essayist and poet, Octavio Paz, from declaring that neither Spain nor Mexico had an enlightenment. In *Los Hijos del Limo* (Children of the Mire), Paz's essential comparative essay on the asymmetries of Europe and Latin-American periodization, he states that Spain had 'ni razón critica ni revoluciones burguesas' ('neither critical reason nor bourgeois revolutions') ... And Mexico, according to Paz, followed Spain in having missed a critical philosophy consonant with the European definition of Enlightenment (*PMLA*, 128, 3, 691).

However, Zamora goes on to cite another Mexican literary historian, Gonzalo Celorio, who contradicts Paz, believing Mexico had a Baroque period: "Celorio's analysis reflects the critical recuperation and revalidation of the New World baroque as a historical period and, more importantly, as a cultural ideology" (*PMLA*, 692). But while this controversy about periodisation continued, one commentator, Eugenio d'Ors, took a different perspective, a tour of the Prado museum:

> As we accompany d'Ors on his visit, then, we imagine ourselves in surroundings very different from those of today's Prado. Moving from room to room, d'Ors observes affinities among artists and makes connections among frames—often unexpected ones, between Poussin and Goya, for example. It is as if the stroll itself—his own kinetic activities, his spatial displacements—allowed him to intuit cultural and aesthetic relations in their 'multinuclear scheme'. He disrupts historical progression and succession, rethinks causes and consequences, in order to play freely with time. So in his walk through the Prado, d'Ors exercises his predilection for

untied fragments, multiple meanings, and comparative possibilities (*PMLA*, 694).

In short, d'Ors intuitive tour of his imaginary Prado replaces progression by way of traditional historical periods—thus violating or ignoring the historical tour set up by the Prado and other similar museums—with an evolution by way of many categories including genres. This innovation influenced a museum exhibit in Houston, Texas nearly a century later. Zamora describes this museum as follows:

> In 2012-13 there was an exhibition of the Museum of Fine Arts Houston of more than one hundred works from the Prado … . The Prado's curator struggled to do exactly what d'Ors did in his three-hour tour in the museum in 1922: break up the match of decades and dynasties. Works were grouped according to genres and themes (religious, historical, and mythological scenes, court and bourgeois portraits, still lives, landscapes, genre scenes), and several paired works were hung side by side to show similarities, differences, influences and shared techniques across centuries. The result was a shared satisfying eccentricity, where painters created their precursors, Borges-d'Ors style, and viewers were encouraged to create traditions of their own (*PMLA*, 694-95).

Zamora concludes that while groups and divisions are needed there are alternatives to the traditional large or overarching categories suitable to regions or mini-periods or eras in-between like the Baroque: the eccentric periods she proposes involve more attention to individual works, their similarities and differences across historical ages on the basis of what she calls themes and genres. I am not sure about the utility of eccentric periods; in its most refined form a period would become particular, the general approaching the specific, defeating the object of periods, that is, large segments of history. Any period concept of use, by definition, must to some extent dwarf or encompass the local and the concrete. Rather, Zamora's research and experience with art exhibitions suggests that individual artists and genres evolve in different ways and at various rates of change, like different members of a family, all of whom are affected by their surroundings, in this instance, a literary period or a spirit of the age, but in ways as different as their various personalities and lifestyles. Nonetheless, Zamora makes an important point about how the local, often lost in the larger period, comes to life in the context of genre: Cohen suggests that instead of eccentric or local periods, we use genre as a basis for revising periods to accommodate different developmental patterns of genres. In particular, Cohen's distinction between innovation or revolution and variation is useful here: "the changes within a period are not revolutionary but are variations, alterations of what is generally accepted" (Rowlett, 249). Zamora's concern for the local requires, Cohen suggests, a careful analysis of variation.

The function of locality and the local is very important in Tarantino's *Once Upon a Time in Hollywood*, 2019. The camera pauses to focus upon the address "Ciello Drive", where the main protagonist, Rick Dalton (Leonardo di Caprio) lives because that street is where the Charles Manson murder occurred; in fact, this infamous house is next to that of Rick. In addition, on a number of occasions we are given the date of occurrences in the film, all in February 1969, just six months before the murder of Sharon Tate and her fellow occupants at the home of Roman Polanski, a very well-known filmmaker who was at the time in Europe. Specific place and time are crucial to understanding this film.

The genre of *Once Upon a Time in Hollywood* is also quite specific, an example of a recent sub-genre concerned with a look back at the Hollywood movie-making world of the 1940-70s when one of the early alternatives to Hollywood was found in Italy where spaghetti westerns became popular. Not coincidentally, Rick is lured into a lucrative contract to shoot some of these films in Italy. We have already seen that *Stan and Ollie* belongs in this sub-genre as do a number of other recent movies, most obviously *Judy*, a portrayal of Judy Garland's life and career during this period. However, Tarantino combines his somewhat nostalgic look back at Hollywood with allusions to the Charles Manson murders, most notably in the film when one of the murderers turns up at the home of Polanski asking for him, only to be told that he is away in Europe. How the world of Rick Dalton and his double/ stunt man Cliff Booth (Brad Pitt) relates to the world of Sharon Tate and the Manson murders is a question posed by this generic combination.

Rick is what in those days would have been known as a B actor, one of a number of little-known minor talents who eked out a living taking many similar parts of the same genre or type—in Rick's case that of the bad guy in B westerns. Cliff, Rick's double. stuntman, driver, and odd-job man has become a friend. Together, they share life in the underworld of Hollywood, the realm of wannabes and those who do wardrobe, make-up, and set-design from trailers in vacant, desert-like locations far from the glamour of Beverly Hills. But they are often loyal friends and can count on one another. On one occasion when Cliff is driving, Rick notices in the car next to them, Roman Polanski and Sharon Tate. Rick is wide-eyed and awe-struck at what for him are A types. But while Rick struggles in this hard world to make it, Sharon Tate seems from his point of view to have made it. And the fact that these two B types are played by Leonardo di Caprio and Brad Pitt suggests that even those at the top could have ended up like Rick and Cliff. Notice here the shift in generic hierarchy, Brad Pitt and Leonardo di Caprio, very much A players, taking the parts of B players.

By contrast, Sharon Tate (Margot Robbie) appears happy in her success and utterly vacant; she seldom speaks, a mute portrait of complacency. The one scene focusing on her involves her trip—admitted for free because she announces that she is in the film—to the movies to see herself: she seems enraptured by her own performance. By this means, Tarantino explains how a man like Manson, a young musician treated with contempt by Polanski, would seek revenge by murdering his girlfriend.

But that does not happen in this film; it is a future crime prepared for by this film. While Sharon Tate enjoys life floating on the drug of success, Rick is striving to fight alcoholism and the increasing inability to remember his lines. Enter Mr. Schwarz (Al Pacino), the movie promoter—someone we would expect to have dealt with the likes of Samuel Goldwyn and Hal Roach. Pacino is brilliant in his cameo part as the movie middleman who sells Rick on spaghetti westerns. He completes the deal not by glamorising Italian westerns but by reviewing Rick's likely future. As a known bad guy, Rick will be knocked out, eliminated, or crushed by all the good guys including perhaps in the end Batman. The result is that Rick is not merely the actor who plays the bad guy but is seen as the bad guy himself. And that according to Schwartz means the end of his career. So Rick goes off to Italy for six months, makes good money, and returns with an Italian bride.

Now recognising himself as a has-been in the industry, Rick decides to sell his house in the Hollywood hills, go to the suburbs, buy a family house and settle down. But unfortunately, he can no longer afford Cliff, so they agree to part after an all-night party. In this final scene the subplot joins with the main plot. The subplot involves Cliff's visit to the previous shooting location of his past films where a group of hippies now live with the owner, an acquaintance of Cliff's. Worried that the owner is being taken advantage of by the hippies, Cliff insists on seeing him. During the visit, one of the hippies punctures his tire. Cliff then beats the hippy until he agrees to fix the tire. Now, some time after that event, a group of the hippies armed with a gun and some knives return for revenge. The result is a blood bath in which the hippies are killed and Cliff, slightly wounded, is taken away in an ambulance.

In a brief coda after this violent scene, Rick is invited next door by Sharon Tate for a drink; the movie ends with a distant shot of them conversing in front of Polanski's house. The suggestion is that the violent scene at Rick's place will be replayed later that same year at the home of Polanski and Sharon Tate. This time, the B team; next time, the A team. The hippies, presumably high on some drug, decided to murder Rick because he, the gun-slinging bad guy, taught them to resort to violence. But this position is hardly that of Tarantino. The hippy attempt at revenge is farcical. Unarmed Cliff laughs at them, sets his dog on them, kills two of the hippies armed with a gun and two knives. However pathetic, the hippies represent the violence in the underbelly of Hollywood, but it is local and specific to those who work with and around the stars. The successful actors seem to float above the rest who struggle with frustrated ambition, like Rick, or earn a minimum wage, like Cliff, serving the others. One of the most poignant scenes in this regard is Cliff on the roof of Rick's house adjusting his TV aerial, looking into the bedroom of Sharon Tate, swaying to music, completely lost in her own world. Only people close to the stars can fully understand the frustration and envy of watching the high life from below.

In terms of genre study, this period piece has what Zamora might characterise as an eccentric ending, one which is particularly localized in time and place, within a few months of and next door to the site of the Manson murders. Considering it in relation to another member of this sub-genre, *Stan and Ollie,* the specificity of the Manson murder is unique. Laurel and Hardy are reconciled in the end but they are getting too old and unwell (Ollie) to continue on tour. The conclusion focuses upon the relationship that developed between the two, a deep sort of tough love and respect that sustained them against the exploitation of Hal Roach and others who made their fortune by way of the great comic partnership.

Rick and Cliff form a similar loyal friendship without the disagreements that punctuated the life of Stan and Ollie, and each tried in his own way to defend and encourage the other. As Cliff says at the beginning of the film when asked if he is a friend of Rick's, "I try to be." But the defence against violence is particular to Hollywood; Stan and Ollie do not confront anything like that on their tours abroad. The Hollywood period piece sub-genre has localised differences that are of historical interpretive significance. Ollie died in 1957 and Stan never worked on stage or screen again; their partnership is what was important for both of them. Rick and Cliff survive. Rick uses his flame thrower against one of the hippies and is delighted to get his friend medical help and go next door for a drink with a star.

Genre and sub-genre hierarchy show us a period shift from the days of Laurel and Hardy when studio moguls controlled and manipulated actors like big industrialists making vast fortunes while paying wages below the market value to most of their employees. But by the late 1960s, alternatives like Italian spaghetti westerns opened up outside of Hollywood where movies could be made at less expense. The studios were sold off for the land because films could be made in other locations with modern technology. The fact that the hippies live on a ranch previously used for movies makes this plain. The unchanged element—the mainstay of the sub-genre—the star system is still in place but is now controlled, not by the big studios, but by power brokers like Harvey Weinstein. Wherever the films are shot, Rick and Cliff remain B actors with the equivalent of Brad Pitt and Leonardo di Caprio above them in the hierarchy.

But Tarantino is suggesting that the difference between these two pairs involves a great deal more than their talent and training.

Powers like those of Weinstein lurk behind; in fact, Tarantino had to sever his connection with Weinstein after the allegations against him became widely known. Is this new era of movie-making, from the 1970s onward, comprised of new forms of power, owing less to the Hollywood-corporate types and more to those with personal influence? This trend is just emerging now with the #Me-Too generation involving allegations against Harvey Weinstein, Donald Trump, Prince Andrew, and others. Under these new conditions even Brad Pitt and Leonardo di Caprio may be vulnerable.

To return briefly to the problem that Zamora raises about genre as an alternative to large overarching period concepts, we could consider *Once upon a Time in Hollywood* based upon the premise that B western movies are a thing of the past. Cliff's world of "shoot 'em ups" is over; the television and film days of Hopalong Cassidy, Tom Mix and Gene Autry have no present-day equivalent. Film and television programmes have moved on, to be replaced by, among others, movies about the Hollywood process behind those films, a sign of period norm innovation. Among this genre we could place *Stan and Ollie, Judy,* and *Once Upon A Time in Hollywood,* all of which present this world dominated by the likes of Hal Roach and Samuel Goldwyn. But the sub-genres within the group develop at a different pace. In comic duos, the move from Laurel and Hardy to Abbott and Costello is a good example of variation, while B westerns simply die out, a negative example of innovation. This kind of uneven historical development will be considered in greater detail in the next chapter.

Here we note that, if innovation and variation of genres are taken into account, the limitations of traditional periods become apparent: we should be able to devise alternative periodic concepts that do not neglect the local and the eccentric. But Zamora's argument in favour of local, eccentric periods seems to me self-defeating: the usefulness of periods is that they encompass large enough segments of history to expose prevalent and persistent norms. A local period, such as a Hollywood mogul era, would be of very limited utility. Typical of members of a genre, the three films that we have considered develop in very different ways, as we have seen, and arrive at different conclusions. Yet they all belong in the same period because responding to the big studio world of Hollywood of the mid twentieth century. Localizing the period does not help make clear the distinction between these members of the genre. Nevertheless, periods are essential in describing change—the basis of any form of interpretation—because they provide the touchstone for defining change from what. The problem is that periods are governed by historical norms which develop in a different way from genres: periods are mainly subject to cultural evolution while genres, also influenced by cultural forces, are subject to artistic and interpretive aims that may resist prevalent social norms. We can begin to develop period concepts that accommodate generic means of development by understanding more precisely how genres develop. In the next chapter I use the concept of the rhizome to suggest how genres develop and how that form of artistic evolution relates art to life.

Chapter Six

After Cohen: New Directions for Genre

I Vlastimil Zuska, "Towards A Cognitive Model of Genre: Genre as a Vector Categorization of Film", *Theoria: An International Journal*, 15, 3, 39, 2000, 481-495 (VZ) and *The Irishman: I Heard you Paint Houses*, directed and produced by Martin Scorsese, 2019.

II Svend Erik Larson, "Landscape, Identity, and War", *NLH*, 35, 2004, 3, 469-490 and *1917*, directed by Sam Mendes, 2019.

III James D. Lilley, "Henry Mackenzie's Ruined Feelings: Romance, Race, and the Afterlife of Sentimental Exchange", *NLH*, 38, 2007, 4, 649-664 and *Cats*, directed by Tom Hooper, 2019.

The idea of this chapter derives from a cryptic suggestion by John Rowlett in his introduction to *Genre Theory and Historical Change: Theoretical Essays of Ralph Cohen, 2017*:

> A Ralph Cohen essay, albeit directional, does not end in a conclusive destination, but opens up, in the language of Deleuze and Guattari, a mapping of rhizomatic connections—and disconnections (Rowlett, xxi).

My purpose is to suggest that Deleuze and Guattari's concept of the rhizome enables us to understand how Cohen's theory of genre can be extended beyond literary criticism and literary history. The ultimate assumption of this chapter involves moving beyond literature: as Cohen asserts that changes of genres are related to cultural history, so cultural history can be influenced by changes of genre.

To do him justice, Cohen does point in this direction:

> Genre study is more than another approach to literature or to social institutions or social practices; it analyses our procedures for acquiring and accumulating knowledge, including the changes that such knowledge undergoes (*NLH*, 34, 2, v).

But Cohen did not pursue the relation of genre theory to the acquisition and accumulation of knowledge in general. Rowlett speaks eloquently of this problem:

> [Cohen's] experimental, journalistic method resulted in essays, seminars, and presentations full of explosive insights, whether clarifying the views of others or carefully and systematically shaping those of his own. Yet setting aside the cognitive difficulty, the lack of widespread appropriation of his revisionary theory can best be accounted for, I suggest, by the lack of a comprehensive source to serve as an explanatory model of his concepts (Rowlett, xix).

This chapter is intended to serve as a further extension of the "explanatory model of his concepts" in the previous chapters and of the future directions for that model.

I) Vlastimil Zuska, "Towards A Cognitive Model of Genre: Genre as a Vector Categorization of Film", *Theoria: An International Journal,* 15, 3, 39, 2000, 481-495 (VZ) and *The Irishman: I Heard you Paint Houses,* directed and produced by Martin Scorsese, 2019.

For purposes of understanding Vlastimil Zuska's essay only the basic concept of the rhizome will be pertinent. Deleuze and Guattari use the image of the rhizome to distinguish a form of development different from that of the traditional linear model, that of root to tree. In addition to growing upward, the rhizome grows laterally. Zuska employs the term "vector" to suggest alternative means of direction and connection by way of angles from 90 to 180 degrees, rather like the missiles from cartoon spaceships miraculously darting at all angles. Cohen makes use of a similar notion when he points out that traditional literary periods do not account for the different kinds of development of various genres; like the lateral roots of the rhizome, genres do not always grow directly upward or progress at the same rate. The ballad may suddenly emerge from centuries of obscurity underground, as it were, while the epic may disappear from the surface without any sign of new growth for centuries. Of course, Cohen is not suggesting that genres can evade history; rather, to revert again to Hans R. Jauss' image of the planets within the solar system, genres are all affected by history, the encompassing galaxy, but in various ways and with different rates of growth or development.

Zuska applies the concept of the rhizome to genre, focusing upon film but, as he makes clear, the principle has applicability to literature and the other arts:

> Traditionally, from Aristotle to the present day, the notion of genre has been considered to have a certain function that transcends particular works or the 'space'

that they occur in, a space that allows certain kinds
of acts and excludes others... [Moreover,] genre is
basically independent of any medium, and is therefore
artistically above any particular kind of art. We know,
for example, the horror story in literature, horror and
mystery horror movies, horror theatre (Grand Guignol),
comics. Because of that superior nature of genre, it is
hardly an act of violence to the film genre to turn to
literary theory, philosophy (of language), and, ultimately,
to cognitive science (problems of categorization and
conceptualization), and the philosophy of mind, for some
genre determinations (VZ, 483).

Zuska believes genres are categories that cross disciplines
and transcend individual works of art. He therefore sees the
problem of film genre as intimately bound up with literary theory
and with the problem of how categories like genres relate to
cognition. We can anticipate then that the goal of this essay is
to relate genre to knowledge: "Genre, genre understanding, and
knowledge of genre are thus not only a matter of encyclopaedic
taxonomy or distributive practice but also an essential condition
of meaningfulness" (VZ, 384).

The definition of genre that Zuska finds most useful for his
project involves "horizons of expectations". This key phrase of
reception aesthetics enables Zuska to connect genre with cognitive
learning. Deleuze and Guattari's concept of the rhizome becomes
a metaphor for how the brain makes sense of or learns about the
world.

In other words, the reception of the film, including
its ever changing categorization, corresponds to the
function of the brain as it was determined by Deleuze
and Guattari: the rhizomatic network forms horizontal

connections, intertextual interconnections, and change (resonances) in the field of genre; vertical integration (that is, the thing which connects different films) then forms the genre field or, in short, a plane of immanence, which is again horizontally connected with other genres (genre fields) and so on (VZ, 488).

For Zuska, the image of the rhizome of knowledge permits the mind to make both horizontal, vertical, and, between the two, vector connections, which includes thinking in both synchronic and diachronic terms. When we first see a new model of a car we know at once that it is, say, a Ford, and yet not the same as last year's Ford, or so Ford hopes. Any specific example of a genre is connected to or is a member of a genre, or more often genres, while at the same time different from other members of the genre or genres, whether that difference involves what Cohen calls variation or innovation. These various connections that Zuska calls vectors include the vertical and the horizontal, and he recognises that they can form a new genre or sub-genre, an innovation, or frame a unique variation of an existing genre or genres.

Consequently, genre can be understood as a multidimensional space which is interwoven with vector sequences, the intersections, knots or clusters, and is activated by gradual vector categorization during the reception of a film. To put it metaphorically, the fly of a particular work is thus trapped in the spider-web or milieu or plane of immanence (VZ, 292-93).

The spider-web trap is temporary, a moment for the mind to take a snapshot, to grasp some meaning, before the stream of time and new examples of the genre alter the picture. This multiple movement of the mind—horizontal, vertical and angles or vectors in between them—sees the work of art as a singular entity while simultaneously understanding its relationship to similar works in the past. Indeed, as Cohen points out, nothing new is comprehended without reference to the old; all knowledge involves the intermingling of similarity and dissimilarity. The difference between the growth process of the rhizome and that of the tree is crucial. The form of the tree is determined by its root; change requires grafting or hybridization, altering the root, as elementary for Aristotle as the fact that acorns produce oak trees, not elms. But the image of the rhizome—and it is only an image, for rhizomes are also determined by their roots—suggests something closer to how we perceive art as a relation of difference, uniqueness from similarity, as in a novel like *Ulysses* that radically changes the novel as a genre. To illustrate how this rhizomatic principle of interpretation alters our perception of a work of art I turn now to Scorsese's *The Irishman: I Heard You Paint Houses*.

I shall focus on the map in the film for it is a linear projection of the main story. From the very beginning, the map is used to plan the trip that Frank (Robert de Niro), Russell (Joe Pesci), and their wives make to Detroit to attend the wedding of Bill's (Ray Romano) daughter. The map itself dates the film very effectively, as does the Lincoln Continental that is driven, a large gas-guzzler of the 1950s, 60s, and 70s, well before satellite navigation systems and smart phones. And Frank's use of the magnifying glass to trace his route indicates his age, now approaching retirement.

The map, it seems to me, represents the old generic method, the root-tree system that would view the film as a Mafia tale about what happens to the few in the gang who survive into old age and what their retirement entails. But the map is not a reliable guide. In fact, Frank, to his surprise, is told not to go to Detroit but to drive to Clinton, Ohio and fly into Detroit, then return by plane to Clinton to complete the drive to Detroit. We are left to wonder about the underground lateral roots of the rhizome that led to this decision; how many gang members were consulted and agreed to this roundabout route. Subsequently we learn that Russell insisted upon this circuitous route to protect Frank and his family from suspicion, anticipating the investigation of the murder of Jimmy Hoffa (Al Pacino). Unlike the flat map, a linear projection like a tree-root system, the film is structured more like a rhizome; the plateau or system of vectors between Clinton, Ohio and Detroit, is a bundle of interrelations that distinguishes this film from other Mafia movies.

The killing of Hoffa—call it murder, assassination or execution—is a distinctive feature of this film, since Hoffa is not really a member of the Mafia. He is finally eliminated by the Mafia because he is more loyal to his union than to the Mafia, even though he recognises that the union could not exist without Mafia support. However corrupt, Hoffa is a union man and his death can be said to mark the beginning of the gradual decline of union power in the United States. Notice now that our analysis has moved from the vertical tree, the Mafia movie, to a horizontal vector—American unions of the period 1950-75, what Cohen calls cultural or social history.

As the first part of the title suggests, although not a member of the then largely Italian Mafia, 'The Irishman' is supported by the Mafia and is closely bound up with their activities. But the difference between Frank, a member of the Mafia, and Jimmy is seen in Frank's daughter Peggy's (Anna Paquin) attitude to the two men. She is ill at ease with her father and with Russell, both Mafiosi, but clearly likes Jimmy, for, as Frank points out, she does not associate him with the violence that is characteristic of both her father and Russell. Hoffa mediates between the underworld and the establishment. Indeed, while Bobby Kennedy tried ceaselessly to convict him, Nixon pardoned him.

Another vector or horizontal plateau in the film is history, involving, specifically, television news telecasts of the main events of the period, from the election of Jack Kennedy, then Bobby Kennedy's investigation of the Teamsters Union, the death of Jack Kennedy, to Watergate and the resignation of Nixon. These events directly affect Jimmy Hoffa more than the Mafia continuing with its usual activities even while Hoffa is sent to prison. The film thus suggests that, given the nature of United States culture at the time, some unions could not exist without some underworld financial backing. In that sense, Peggy is right. However implicated with the gang, Jimmy is not wholly a part of it, and the goals of the union are not the same as those of the Mafia. As Jimmy points out to Tony Pro (Stephen Graham) when both are in prison, the union contract makes a distinction between those convicted of fraud and those with intent to commit bodily harm. The result is that Hoffa keeps his pension and Tony forfeits his; that is the law and even Hoffa can do nothing about the law. For union contracts are based upon law.

But to understand the function of the union during this period in the USA we must turn to the life of Frank, who at the end of the film is living on his union pension but unreconciled with his daughter. The subtitle, *I Heard You Paint Houses*, is at this point pertinent. The phrase is code for being willing to do assassinations. And, as Frank adds at one point, I also do my own carpentry, meaning disposal of the body. Yet Frank did not begin as a mobster, but as the typical teamster; we see him early in the film driving a truck that breaks down. At the nearby gas station he meets Russell who in turn introduces him to Bill (Ray Romano), the lawyer. These two vectors or lateral connections lead to Frank's becoming a member of the Mafia and having in the end to execute his friend and respected leader, Jimmy Hoffa, an element of the film that is fictional since no one knows how Hoffa died. Why does Frank have to kill Jimmy? Because he knows that if he does not he himself will be eliminated and his family will be vulnerable.

Frank is essentially a soldier, a veteran of World War II, who obeys his orders and faces the problems that arise in carrying them out. Near the end of his life we see Frank in his usual matter-of fact way choosing his casket and burial place. He is a downright man who knows that, as he tells Jimmy, "it is what it is". In short, the world of a Teamsters Union man at that time was a rhizome of union principle and laws and underworld money. The working stiff had to accept that and live with it. Frank had to think like a rhizome, attending to Jimmy and the establishment powers above him while being equally responsive to Russell and the gang members who will guarantee the protection of his family.

By contrast, Jimmy perished by the tree principle, insisting that he was synonymous with the union, looking only upward, neglecting the vectors of the gang coming at him sideways. Frank survives without expressing contrition although accepting some priestly mercy and refusing to give any evidence against the Mafia members even though they are now all dead. For Frank what he did was necessary to survive and to protect his family, facts of life that deserve neither praise nor forgiveness. Frank's world is the rhizome of the union culture of his day: survival was all. He hoped his daughters would understand, but as one of them explains they were afraid to ask him for help lest he would violently overreact as in the incident with the grocer who for pushing Peggy ended up with a crushed hand. But history has placed Frank between Jimmy and Russell, leaving the door open like Hoffa and remaining tight-lipped like Russell.

The Irishman focuses upon Frank because his survival is a microcosm of the structure of the film. An able truck driver, Frank always looks at once straight ahead and to his side mirrors; the film also combines the union hierarchy—straight ahead or upward with the Mafia lateral control demonstrating that the Teamsters Union could not survive without Mafia backing, In generic terms, I would suggest that instead of a Mafia movie, *The Irishman* is about the beginning of the demise of union power in the United

States because, among other things, it was associated with the corrupt power of the Mafia. Bobby Kennedy went after one of the lateral roots of the Teamsters Union, the Mafia connection, but inadvertently weakened the unions in general: perhaps he shared with Hoffa the inability to think rhizomatically.

The decision about the genre of *The Irishman* involves the rhizomatic roots, both upward and lateral, of the artistic goals of the film and the social norms of the time. But the social norms themselves are more clearly historical. Having grown up in this period, my memory is that while the finances of most unions were not very transparent, the Teamsters Union was considered more corrupt than most and that is probably why Bobby Kennedy went after Hoffa. But the new insight provided by the movie is that while Kennedy failed to indict Hoffa, he may have inadvertently begun the demise of union power in the United States. In the next section, I extend the concept of the rhizome beyond the individual work to genre and genre theory.

II) Svend Erik Larson, "Landscape, Identity, and War", *NLH*, 35, 3, 469-490 and *1917*, directed by Sam Mendes, 2019.

In this section, I shall demonstrate that the rhizomatic conception of genre leads beyond the literary in a psychological sense, to show that the landscape of war relates to our identity. Svend Erik Larson begins with what he calls the obvious that is less than obvious:

> War takes place in a landscape called a battlefield, and the aim of war is to exercise control over a landscape designated as territory. This widespread view is as trivial as it sounds. The conclusion goes without saying: in the real world, war and landscape are necessarily linked to each other like Siamese twins. On a symbolic level literature

can interpret this relationship and also make it essential, a relation in the very nature of war (*NLH*, 35, 3, 469).

Larson goes on to explain that what is essential to the literature that links war and landscape is not describing lost beauty or the destructiveness of the environment that is the inevitable result of modern war. Rather, literature "investigates the possibilities, the modalities, and the conditions of a relationship" that for Larson constitute "the cultural interpretation of human life" (*NLH*, 35, 3, 470). This claim for the cultural significance of war is presented in three stages; 1) changing concepts of war, 2) changing concepts of nature, and 3) cultural identity that results from war.

From the classical period until the mid-nineteenth century war had little relation to cultural identity.

> Whether the landscape is destroyed, left in its natural state, or perceived as something with its own identity, such occurrences are never part of the representation of war as a quest for identity ... . The reason is simple: landscape and cultural identity are not mutually interdependent ... But from the nineteenth century onwards this martial attitude has been reversed or at least contested. Landscape as interpreted by literature plays an important role in the transformation of values (*NLH*, 35, 3, 475).

The second major change involves concepts of nature. During the classical period and the Renaissance, nature serves as a stereotypical background for war, as a sign or omen of its outcome. But the turn to aesthetics in the Renaissance coupled with the rise of science later contribute to an altered view of the landscape of war by bringing to the fore individual perceptions or concrete points of view. Once viewpoint is established, war becomes a much more ambiguous matter. Larson explains this paradox:

War is on the one hand an unfolding of human power and heroism, but when most successful it is at the same time a destruction of the landscape where this power has to unfold. It is in this marriage between science and aesthetics that the modern anti-heroic attitude to war was born (*NLH*, 35, 3, 480).

From this point onward, according to Larson, landscape and war shape our national identity, bringing us to the third change, involving cultural identity.

Thus a modern landscape is always an ambiguous sign of war and peace, only accessible in fragments on the conditions of individual perception and aesthetic distance, and thus revealing both individual power and weakness … . We are left with a permanent uneasiness in the literary description of landscape, an uneasiness that in itself is synonymous with war (*NLH*, 35, 3, 486).

Larson concludes that major change in the cultural meaning of the relationship between war and landscape provides two functions for literature: 1) While older literature idealised war, modern literature should devote itself to a portrayal of the concrete character of war and the "actual conditions for human identity in relation to the problems of place and bodily existence". 2) Moreover, literature can "remind us that the real landscapes with real bloodshed and real persons, only reach us through the arbitrary and abstract constructions which are circulated by the media"(*NLH*, 35, 3, 488).

Although not using the language of genre, Larson is describing the progress of a sub-genre, war landscape, that is derived from descriptive genres that go back to Virgil's *Georgics*, Chaucer's description of the garden of January and May, Milton's *Lycidas*,

Denham's *Cooper's Hill*, Pope's *Windsor Forest*, not to mention the nature description found in the novels and poetry of the last two centuries. The terms employed by Larson, those of cultural change, serve to remind us of Cohen's insistence that genres and genre change are intimately related to cultural change. What is of particular interest for our present purpose is how Larson demonstrates in his conclusion that the literature of war shapes not only our attitude to war but also our cultural identity.

The description of the war genre here is again rhizomatic; the movement from classical times up to the nineteenth century is essentially tree-like in that cultures show little interest in the collateral damage war wreaks upon the landscape. In the nineteenth century, according to Larson, concern for the damage to the natural surroundings becomes important, and in time a new question arises. In addition to war seen traditionally as the protection of the nation, the question is now raised as to what war does to the culture of the nation. Larson sees an innovation in the genre. The rhizome of the war genre shows us the collateral damage of war not only to the landscape but also to our culture, particularly to how our culture's media represent war to us.

To illustrate this concept, I turn from literature to film, fast becoming the literature of our culture. Sam Mendes' *1917* is a journey of identity on a single day, April 6, 1917, when two British soldiers are sent on a near-impossible mission to cross no-man's land and the enemy lines to warn two battalions, some 1600 men, of a trap set by the Germans that will result in certain slaughter. The historical accuracy of this account does not seem to be an issue. Judging from the dedication of the film to Lance Corporal Alfred Mendes, the grandfather of the director, the story derives from a veteran of battle: the point seems to be that what happens is probable or believable—certainly it was to the soldiers on the front line—which of course tells us as much about our culture and what we find believable as about the war itself a century earlier.

Lance Corporal Tom Blake (George MacKay) is chosen by his superior because his brother is one of the soldiers to be ambushed if his battalion is not warned. He is told to take one companion with him and chooses his best friend, Lance Corporal Will Schofield (Dean-Charles Chapman). The more seasoned and experienced of the two soldiers, Will is more wary of this suicide mission, but since Tom insists that they must try to save his brother, Will reluctantly agrees, not out of respect for the official order but in loyalty to his friend.

The journey, as harrowing as anyone could imagine, involves landscape and cultural identity. But, in the end, we see how the two are related so that the film, like the literature Larson describes, shows an element of our cultural identity, that is, it extends beyond the realm of art to that of reality. Involving very limited landscape, the first stage takes us along the trenches of mud, corpses, wounded and tense soldiers. Reaching the front line, crossing into enemy territory, Will wants to turn back, but Tom suggests he may earn a medal. Will points out that he already received a medal at the battle of the Somme that he traded for a glass of wine because he was thirsty. Here in the midst of a landscape barren but for craters of death, remnants of trees without leaves or branches, we understand Will's disillusionment with war and particularly with this futile mission. We are reminded of the *Beyond the Fringe* sketch in which Perkins is sent on a similar mission. Upon leaving, he says, "Au revoir," to his superior officer who replies, "No, Perkins, adieu."

But the young soldiers persist and arrive at the abandoned trenches of the enemy that are very similar to their own, except now eerily empty. The audience and the two soldiers see the battle from the point of view of the enemy, and it does not at first appear very different from the view on the other side. However, it is booby-trapped and they narrowly escape with their lives. Tom is quite shocked but, more alert, Will, fortunately spots the tripwire. The landscape has become more varied with bombshell craters, corpses and various parts of bodies—Golgotha, the hell of war. As Larson suggested, no attempt is made to disguise or cover up the full horror of war.

But once behind the front line, a cherry orchard in full bloom is visible in a deserted farmyard. As they approach closer it becomes clear that the trees have been cut down, even though in full bloom. The cultural question is again, would the British have done the same. Tom is shocked to see cows have been shot; Will takes it in his stride. Although telling Tom he doesn't like the place, Will stumbles upon a pail of fresh milk from which he drinks and fills his canteen. Shortly thereafter, the two soldiers confront a German aviator whose plane crashes into the barn. Instead of finishing him off, Tom insists that they try to save him. After they drag the pilot from his burning aircraft, the German stabs Tom and Will shoots him. We are left to wonder, would a British pilot have done the same to a German who saved his life? Tom dies in the arms of Will, who promises to try to save Tom's brother. Is the death of Tom the result of cultural difference or of war? Did the German pilot fear torture or merely strike at the enemy as he had been trained to do? The landscape here is what Larson calls ambiguous—fresh milk, beautiful cherry blossom, dead cows, dead trees and now two corpses.

Yet for Will this bitter-sweet location is his turning-point. Now he is consumed, as Tom was before, with his mission, if for nothing else, than to avenge or compensate for the death of his friend. Suddenly, British troops arrive, help him remove Tom's body and offer him a lift. Once he explains his mission to the other soldiers they befriend him and offer him their precious bottle of spirits. Is this British camaraderie or one of the necessities of any nation at war? Even the officer in charge breaks ranks to warn Will that he needs to be aware that Colonel Mackenzie (Benedict Cumberbatch), the commander he needs to find, is a war-monger who will only be stopped if there are witnesses. For a moment an officer and an enlisted man share the danger of battle and the imminent threat of death; the respect of this officer and his men for his mission seems to put steel into Will's spine. We note here the rhizomatic perspective, a lateral move that subverts the hierarchy, when the officer shares with an enlisted man something personal about one of his fellow officers, information, that as we shall see, is crucial to saving he two battalions.

Now that the convoy is stalled, Will goes off on his own toward the city, his final destination, and the landscape changes again. First, Will is nearly killed by a German sniper who seems to prefer death, his own and others, to life rather like, we assume, Colonel Mackenzie. This war psychosis seems to affect both sides from foot soldier to commander. Once he has dispatched the sniper, Will enters a surreal city, a sort of bombed-out movie set, walls and roofless rooms without civilians, and full of snipers, deserters, and/ or prisoners. This urban Golgotha is a mighty maze. By chance, Will hides from pursuit in a room where he discovers a young French woman with an infant. Having assured her that he means no harm to her or the infant, she nurses his wound. He offers them all of his rations, but she explains the child can only take milk. Miraculously he produces his canteen of milk from the farm: the sense of decency that he and Tom manifested at the farm might finally save a life. And Will, seeing the young woman looking after a child that is not her own, feels a renewed determination to save Tom's brother and his comrades. Ambiguity is again present; this location is the last place Will would expect to find a kind young woman and an infant in need of something he is carrying.

But the deadline for the battle is fast approaching, so Will sets off on the final phase of his journey. And again the landscape or waterscape in this instance changes. Dodging snipers, he jumps into a river; the French woman had warned him that the camp he sought was near the river. He barely survives the rushing current taking him over a high cascade, leading him to a calm section. Here, breathless and stunned, he clambers ashore over piles of corpses. Hearing in the distance what sounds like singing in English, he comes upon the British soldiers. They direct him to Colonel Mackenzie who at first dismisses him as a mere soldier. But Will insists that he has a letter from the General. Because other officers are present, Mackenzie reads the letter, then reluctantly orders his men to stand down. Eventually, Will finds Tom's brother, breaks the bad news about Tom, and goes off to rest under a tree—this one surprisingly with branches and leaves. We see him looking at treasured snapshots of his wife and two daughters. Having saved 1600 men from a massacre he has also, in a sense, rejoined his family. At the same time we can still hear ringing in our ears, Colonel Mackenzie's final words to Will after obeying the order to call off the attack, "Fuck off, Schofield." Instead of congratulating Will for saving his men, Mackenzie is frustrated at the interruption of his war games.

Cultural identities are mixed, from suicidal snipers and war-mad commanders to decent soldiers who look after their comrades, friends, and family. *1917* shows us the horrors of war and leaves us with the open question: what will prevail, war-mongering or peaceful decency? What would have happened if Will had not had a letter from the general, if he had only his own words by way of testimony? But the General's letter functions like the genre of war landscape. Mackenzie is forced to see the deadly consequences of war. And we are taken on the long journey of war—and the technique of long takes Mendes insisted upon serves this end— leading us to see that this decision between war and negotiation may be the next crossroads for our culture.

Typically, the rhizomatic generic structure points vertically and horizontally. Mackenzie on top is as obsessed with war as are the desperate, marooned German snipers. And Will is no less moved to help a starving infant than to save the lives of two battalions of his comrades. Now a century later, we are struggling to protect the earth, not from war but global warming. And the same vertical and horizontal obstacles remain: powerful people who refuse to face facts and their loyal followers complacently continuing to pollute the environment.

Moreover, the genre of the landscape of war progresses like a rhizome; *1917* looks at a battle of WWI a century later. The hierarchical tree-root old genre sees another war movie, but Mendes shows us the significance of the lateral movement of exceptional soldiers and officers who, against a mainstream command that had little concern for the foot soldiers, the cannon fodder of war, managed to prevent a massacre. The genre has developed from glorifying war to showing us the heroism of those who prevent an unnecessary massacre. Our cultural identity has changed since the days of WWI, and the genre change is dialectically related to that social change insofar as art responds to life and life responds to art. Larson has described how war relates to our cultural identity, moving from the public to the private; in the next section the point of view is reversed from private to public, from feelings to culture.

III) James D. Lilley, "Henry Mackenzie's Ruined Feelings: Romance, Race, and the Afterlife of Sentimental Exchange", *NLH*, 38, 4, 649-664 and *Cats*, directed by Tom Hooper, 2019.

In this section, I will demonstrate how the genre of sentimental romance refers to reality. James Lilley argues that Marx's *Capital* is structured like a romance. The specific romances Lilley chooses as his examples are two by Henry Mackenzie: *The Man of Feeling* (1771) and *Julia de Roubigné* (1777).

Lilley begins by offering an alternative to the traditional view of romance:

> I show how the sentimental romance produces two qualitatively distinct kinds of affective value: on the one

hand, feeling is valued because it functions as principle of public exchange, enabling the affective subject to participate as a 'man of the world,' in a community or politics of feeling; but at the same time, feeling is also esteemed as a totally private essence, a material fact of the subject's own singular personality and unique homespun history... . I argue that affection's public 'exchange value' and private 'use-value' can each appear and distinguish itself only to the extent that it obscures our view of the other (*NLH*, 649-50).

Rather than promoting the public values of expressing one's feelings and realising them in the public sphere, Lilley focuses on the loss or "ruin" of the inner private element of the subject of sentimental romance. This clash between the public and the private is demonstrated by an analysis of Mackenzie's novels in relation to Marx's *Capital*. Two examples should clarify this position. In *The Man of Feeling*, the protagonist Harley comes upon a destitute beggar, takes pity on him, and gives him some money, reflecting as follows upon the charitable shilling:

Harley had drawn a shilling from his pocket; but virtue made him consider on whom he was going to bestow it. Virtue held back his arm—but a milder form, a younger sister of virtue's ... smiled upon him. His fingers lost their compression—nor did virtue offer to catch the money as it fell. It had no sooner reached the ground than the watchful cur (a trick he had been taught) snapped it up and, contrary to the most approved method of stewardship, delivered it immediately into the hands of his master (*NLH*, 652).

Lilley argues that this anecdote is reminiscent of Marx's table that market forces make dance grotesquely like a wooden four-legged ballerina. Marx used this example to demonstrate that market forces can result in a table being sold or promoted as something quite different than a mere table: for example, as an object of prestige that everyone must own to be truly bourgeois, rather like having a decorative statue of a ballerina. In this episode, the shilling is subject to market forces, rising and falling, moving from man to animal, represented by the beggar and the trick that he has taught his dog for purposes of monetary survival. The man of feeling's private attempt to be charitable is converted by the public world of the market into something quite different, a dog trick. The distance between Harley and the beggar and his cur is increased in spite of the attempt to reach across to him. Lilley explains as follows:

> Economics of affection, like Marx's romance of the commodity, play out the tension between an authentic value (an utterly private feeling) and its subsequent corruption within the public exchange (*NLH*, 653).

Lilley concedes that the man of feeling exemplifies "ruined feeling", unable to bring his inner feelings to satisfactory expression in the world at large.

Turning now to the second of Mackenzie's novels, *Julia de Roubigné*, Lilley demonstrates that Julia considers the problem of private virtue and pubic charity in the context of marriage.

> *Julia de Roubigné* takes the challenge to heart. In its determination to open up ruined space for sentiment in the afterlife of marriage—a space obscured from public view and utterly devoid of the 'sort of happiness' that silences the sentimental narrative—the text goes so far as to insist that the erotics of victimhood and servitude penetrate even the most ideal of marriages (*NLH*, 657).

In short, even the most intense and devoted forms of marital love cannot escape Marxist market forces that will result in some form of sentimentalisation, a sort of Valentine's Day massacre.

Lilley concludes that these novels of sentiment, if read, in a sense, against the grain, expose the ultimate dilemma of private feelings becoming ruined by the dialectical forces of the marketplace. Anything but sentimental, Lilley argues, these tales show the futility of communicating feelings:

> The concept of the community united by universal, public sympathies and a common sentimental currency appears to level differences between human subjects ... . However, as Julia's hyperemotional tear demonstrates, these fragmented and non-valuable tokens are no strangers to the logic of the commodity. If these tokens are to act as currency within the sentimental community, they must be quantifiable: we must be able to possess them to greater or lesser degrees. Instead of democratically leveling differences between people, the sentimental romance singles out and privileges specific moments of exceptional suffering, congealing personal pain into a public token—a thing of ruined feeling (*NLH*, 660).

This Marxist reading of sentimental feeling suggests that we live perforce in a world of public commodification that will undermine the basis of feeling that is by its very nature not a commodity. The process is rhizomatic in that your personal feelings, directed linearly toward someone or something, must be conveyed via some form of communication that will be vectored laterally by Facebook, Twitter, or any of the other forms of social media and may in the process be distorted and misunderstood. This new world of social networking moves well beyond that of Julia de Roubigné.

Cats (2019), directed by Tom Hooper, shows how the ruined or commodified feelings of sentimental romance are related not only to the individual but also to society. Perhaps what is best known about *Cats* (2019) is how badly it was reviewed. Let me begin with a sample of some of the reviews found online:

> The best thing here is that it's at least under two hours.
> Diego Batlle
> *Otroscines.com*

> The film is a triple-decker weirdburger from the twitching ears to the too-long tails that make the ensemble look like lemurs.
> Richard von Busack
> *MetroActive*

> I struggled throughout the movie to not fall asleep.
> William Venegas
> *La Nación* (Costa Rica)

> *Cats'* main sin... is that it is boring.
> María Fernanda Mugica
> *La Nación* (Argentina)

> In the end: *Cats* is a CG [Computer Graphics] horror of weird cat mutants dancing and singing nonsense in weird people-sized settings with no people. Run away.
> *Top Critic*, online

Clearly, most reviewers found the film disturbing, particularly the rendering of the characters in the film as "cat-mutants", that is, not people dressed and acting like cats, but as cat-people. I begin here since it is possible that what many did not like about the film was a mirror image of our society, an unflattering one that we would prefer left unseen. It is well to recall here the central argument of this chapter: while Cohen emphasises that changes of genres are always related to cultural history, I would add that genre change can also lead us to a fuller understanding of cultural history. The genre change involves transforming the stage musical version of *Cats* into a movie of "mutant cats" moving and behaving in feline ways. It is notable in this regard that even the trailer put off many reviewers because the costumes suggested cat-people's genitals, and the facial make-up consisted of whiskers and forehead hair that were seen as grotesque. In addition, magic is introduced. Macavity, the mystery cat (Idris Elba), the most feared and evil of the cats, is capable of "apparating", that is, magicking himself and others away then reappearing out of nowhere. I shall return to the magic element shortly. But for now, it is important to keep in mind that, as one of the more positive reviewers remarked, the critics had their claws out for this movie. The prevailing critical response was cat-like, or, more accurately, Macavity-like.

What sort of cultural changes are suggested by these genre innovations? The Jellicle cats are highly individualised, independent, with distinct personalities. They congregate occasionally in small groups but more often remain alone. The dancing suggests that like street cats they move in their own sphere but are nonetheless constantly aware of the others. Victoria, the white cat (Francesca Howard) the outsider, a mere alley cat, is at first treated warily by the Jellicles, yet she as an outsider helps Grizabella (Jennifer Hudson), the ostracised cat, to be accepted back into the group. Perhaps the key to the portrayal of the cats is the final song when they point out that the only way to define a cat is to say it is not a dog. I wonder whether, if the roles had been changed from cats to dogs, the film would have elicited a similarly negative response from reviewers.

In what sense is our society more like that of cats than dogs? Dogs are pack animals while cats are usually solitary. The Jellicles in the film seem more like a neighbourhood gang than a pack or herd. They randomly come together and part on friendly or antagonistic terms as they wish. For the purposes of the film story they gather together in preparation for the Ball. Is present-day society more like a gang than a dog pack, with more interest in individual independence? Are the heads of our society more like gang leaders than top dogs? Perhaps. If so, it would help explain why the film is so disturbing for many reviewers.

But the main plot involves the competition at the Jellicles Ball for the Jellicle Choice, the one cat that will be selected to go to the Heaviside Layer and be granted a new life. This reward is appropriate in a world of cats in that only one can win. The victor literally ascends heavenward, suggestive of the revival of religion, another feature of our present society. At this point Macavity, a sort of devil figure, puts himself forward for the prize, and when rebuffed, magics away the other competitors. Victoria encourages Mr. Mistoffelees (Laurie Davidson) to use his magical abilities to bring back the other competitors, resulting in the rescue of all except for Macavity, the deep-voiced, big baddy who remains at large like the top members of corrupt establishments in our world.

Various solo performances serve to promote particular cats for the Heaviside Layer, rather like political rallies. Appealing to our lowest instincts, Bambalunna (Taylor Swift), an ally of Macavity, sings and gyrates in an overtly sensual and sexual way, even introducing catnip into the atmosphere. Gus or Asparagus, the theatre cat (Ian McKellen), offers himself as star and subject of a self-drama, an ego trip suggestive of certain contemporary political leaders. But Old Deuteronomy (Judi Dench) is not impressed. Instead she befriends Victoria, assuring her that she will be a Jellicle cat one day and chooses the cat that Victoria favours, Grizabella, in compensation for her suffering a life of ostracism and homelessness on the streets.

In celebration of the recovering of those who have been

apparated and the reentry of Grizabella into the group, Victoria and Mr. Mistoffelees dance together imitating a cat-like mating ritual. In contrast to a traditional dance of celebration, Macavity suddenly reappears, interrupting the ascension of Grizabella to the Heaviside Layer by blocking the rope that is lifting the chandelier heavenward. Finally letting go of the rope, he falls on top of Nelson's column while the other cats watch his descent with glee, resting comfortably on the lion in Trafalgar Square. Clearly, the conclusion is making a statement about British society, however one wishes to formulate it. But the point for our purposes is that, as Lilley suggested with Mackenzie and Marx, there is often a surprising relationship between romance and reality that is clarified by an analysis of how genre change relates to cultural evolution.

In my view, one of the most compelling elements of *Cats* is the singing and dancing. The movement and rhythm are rhizomatic; cats do move in sideways, vector-like darts. The cat-like voice modulation and multi-dimensional, unconventional dance moves seem to operate on multiple axes, a sort of ballet of cat survival, checking one another out. Has the rhizome replaced the tree-root as the emblem of our society? Are our relations with one another less straightforward and more catlike, lateral and less predictable?

Moreover, what we might call the subgenre of *Cats* also proceeds like a rhizome. In 1939, T. S. Eliot published *Old Possum's Book of Practical Cats*, a genial, light, and whimsical group of poems about individual differences, like those of people but a bit more evident to us when expressed in the form of cats. In 1981, the musical version of *Cats* appeared, a great comic success, featuring the charm and beauty of a society tolerating difference and individuality. The film of 2019, in my view, sees individuality in much darker terms, moving in a more tragic, lateral direction from the musical, suggesting a society that is somewhat anti-social. And at this moment when some 40% of the population is in lockdown because they would not heed the advice of medical experts advising them to avoid close contact, the film speaks to our time. Dogs, or so we believe, can be trained to obey – I am not aware of any classes in cat obedience.

The image of the rhizome helps us understand how genre change gradually moves literature toward life because, as Cohen asserts repeatedly, genre relates to the social element of culture. Like a cat it disappears, then reappears, darts in unexpected directions, subject to and affecting its environment, that is, history, changing but somehow maintaining an identity. Maybe we dog-lovers have something to learn from cats.

Finally, the metaphor of the rhizome is helpful with regard to the problem of periodisation. Genres, like cats, move in their own sphere at different rates of development. They interact with one another hierarchically and share subservience to history, but the effect of social and cultural issues varies with each genre. Rather than turning to smaller and more local periods that are of very limited utility, Cohen suggests that we reconfigure the larger period denominations in terms that permit a variety of different kinds and rates of development. For instance, The Age of Reason has been long discarded as it permitted only one kind of change, whereas The Augustan Age suggests a much broader range of kinds of change that are more suitable to generic variation. The task of improving periodisation is, as Micah Mattix argued, accommodating difference. Difference, as Cohen often points out, is at the heart of learning, of knowledge, that is, decisions about what is difference, different from what and why. In my conclusion, I consider how Cohen relates literary analysis to learning in general.

Conclusion

I conclude by examining briefly Cohen's analysis of *Huckleberry Finn* appended at the end of an edition published by Bantam Books in 1965. The title page lists his contribution as follows: "with special aids prepared by RALPH COHEN". These "aids" consist of pages 282-314, placed after the text of the novel and divided into four sections: 1. "Games and Growing Up: A Key to Understanding *Huckleberry Finn*". 2. "Is *Huckleberry Finn* a Great Novel?–Opinions, Reviews, and Comments". 3."*Huckleberry Finn* and *The Catcher in the Rye*". 4. "Mark Twain: A Biographical Sketch".

These materials do not constitute an introduction since presumably the text has already been read when the reader comes to Cohen's special aids. Rather, I suggest, these essays are guides to understanding and interpretation. Moreover, the order of the remarks, with the biographical sketch coming at the end as opposed to at the beginning where it would be expected in an introduction, suggests that Cohen is moving beyond reading to a higher level of interpretation. And characteristically, he begins with the form or shape of the specific work of art that will lead him to genre:

> The form of a book is the way that it is told—-the ideas and actions expressed in a particular order. To understand the form of a story is to understand how it is told as well as what is told (*HF*, 282).

Instead of applying generic laws, rules, or labels, Cohen begins by pointing to what he sees as "key" to understanding the text; "games and growing up", that is, "games, disguises, tricks, and superstitions" that are inherent not only in children's behaviour but also in that of adults. These games can take on a comic or tragic mode; "at some times, an exuberant, comic gaiety; at others, a violent, threatening, somberness" (*HF*, 282).

The games in the story, according to Cohen, can be divided into three sorts, the "childish games" Huck plays with Tom Sawyer in the first section, the "game as disguise" in the middle section enabling Huck to escape from his father and Aunt Sally, and the "game as life," in the final section, when Tom and Huck save Jim from being returned to slavery. The most important point here for Cohen is that games for Tom are simply that, games: he has nothing to lose as a free, white, middle class young boy. Huck, on the other hand, is lower class, subject to the abuse of a violent, prejudiced, and almost permanently inebriated father. In the final and climactic section of the novel it is essential, Cohen believes, to realise that Tom knows what Huck does not, that Jim has already been freed: Huck believes he is breaking the law while Tom takes no such risk. Once this key to the text is understood, the generic terms "picaresque" (295) and "autobiography" (294) are applied to the story. This form of mixed genre has the flexibility, as described above in Chapter One, to accommodate the two different worlds of Tom and Huck, ranging from fantasy to realism and from the comic to the near tragic.

The variation between fantasy and realism, comedy and tragedy highlights the polarity between Tom and Huck, particularly in the final episode. Here the freeing of Jim is for Tom a comic game but involves Huck in the tragedy of being a "low-down abolitionist", behaviour that Huck regards as not only unlawful but also sinful. Cohen's reading of *Huckleberry Finn* involves combining and interrelating these two points of view, illustrating the need to interpret why genres are mixed, as outlined in Chapter Two.

The phrase haunting Huck's conscience—"Alright then, I'll go to hell"—relates to the historical era of *Huckleberry Finn* when, in many states, aiding a runaway slave was a crime and would have been regarded as a sin by many in the society of the time. As was suggested in Chapter Three, historical placement is often crucial to understanding artistic purpose. Slavery laws, for Cohen, serve to test the new-found love of Huck and Jim. Pappy, Huck's father, to say nothing of his cohorts, would undoubtedly have imbued his son with his prejudice against African-Americans and made certain that he was anything but a "slave-lover", let alone an abolitionist. So Huck's love for Jim places him not only against the law forbidding aiding a runaway slave but also violates the social mores opposing friendship with an African-American.

In this respect, the reception of *Huckleberry Finn* at its first publication in 1884 is important. Most disapproved of the language as "trashy" and asserted that the story "degenerates into gross trifling with every fine feeling" (*HF*, 294). These overtly moral and implicitly philosophical and ideological criticisms are countered by Cohen in a defence of the genre of the text.

> Most critics received the book unfavorably, and for reasons unconnected with its artistic aspects. Few seemed aware of the great character painting in the book, its magnificent passages of description, its vigor of style, and the appropriateness of the picaresque structure to the material. Least of all did they recognize the significant Americanism in *Huckleberry Finn*, or if they did sense this quality, it was only to revile it as coarse and vulgar (*HF*, 295).

However, as we saw in Chapter Four, the critic who crosses disciplines—here from literature to moral philosophy—must keep the appropriate genre in mind. As a picaresque autobiography,

Huckleberry Finn uses Huck's language to reflect his inner thoughts: his conscience would hardly ring true in more refined or less "coarse" terms. And the contrast between Huck's personal idiom and the "magnificent passages of description" serves to place the protagonist in a new and unexpected situation. In aiding Jim's struggle for freedom, Huck is as out of his comfort zone as he would be on the Champs-Elysées. His endeavours in this respect take him well beyond any of the games he plays with Tom Sawyer. Another attack upon the tale Cohen cites is an essay designed to show that *Huckleberry Finn* is not a great novel and that Mark Twain should therefore not be compared to Abraham Lincoln:

> The association of Lincoln and Twain may seem appropriate at first glance—but only at first glance … . Insofar as Lincoln the writer and Twain the writer can be compared, Lincoln is the greater. Lincoln's wit, also in the vernacular idiom, is frequently more subtle than Twain's and may be expected to be more lasting. Lincoln's ability in writing analytical prose, flexible and closely reasoned, his ability in writing a serious and, when the occasion required, a solemn rhetoric were also greater than Twain's (*HF*, 303).

Cohen's generic analysis questions this judgment. Twain's vernacular wit had to be appropriate to the character of Huck, surely not comparable to that of a presidential address. Moreover, Twain's novel as a picaresque autobiography cannot be expected to contain prose like that of the "Gettysburg Address". Comparisons that violate genre are of little validity.

Most reviews of *Huckleberry Finn* were negative until well after the general attitude to slavery changed. Interestingly, in 1939, one of the earlier positive reviews focuses upon genre, exemplifying how history and genre are connected, as articulated in Chapter Five:

Huckleberry Finn has the great advantage of being written in autobiographical form. This secures a unity of narration that is most valuable: every scene is given, not described … . While "Tom Sawyer" is scarcely more than an apparently fortuitous collection of incidents, and its thread has to do with murders, this story has to do with a more intelligible plot. Huckleberry runs away from his worthless father, and floats down the Mississippi on a raft, in company with Jim, a runaway Negro. This plot gives great opportunity for varying incidents (*HF*, 294).

The genre change described above, from that of *Tom Sawyer*, "an apparently fortuitous collection of incidents", to autobiography serves to move from the episodic quality of the earlier work to the sense of personal responsibility on the part of Huckleberry Finn. The most famous scene in the book focuses upon Huck facing the most momentous decision of his life. Alone on the river or on Jackson Island, Huck and Jim get along well as friends, but soon interference from society takes the form of the law enforcers looking for the run-away slave: Huck is confronted with the question of whether or not to lie to save his friend from being arrested by the police. Cohen describes this moment as follows:

Caught in this net, the young boy and the decent man are surrounded either by corrupt people who are lawless, by people who insist on 'playing the game' by the given rules like Tom or Aunt Polly, or by aristocratic tyrants who make their own rules, or by helpless innocents who don't know what the world is like. With such choices the decent man can only do what Huck does: loving Jim and placing his trust in this love rather than in proper laws, he prepares to break the laws and 'go to Hell.' In one of the most moving passages in the book, he makes the choice between human values and legal values, with the full awareness of the consequences. He chooses 'wickedness,' and he chooses the consequences of it (*HF*, 289).

Cohen's commentary here involves the move beyond the literary suggested in Chapter Six, that he often pointed to without characterising in detail. The phrase, "hopeless innocents who don't know what the world is like" is a version of "nous", or a more penetrating form of common sense, a sort of knowledge of the world that recalls Samuel Johnson's remark that "life must be seen before it can be known". Cohen characterises this knowledge as cultural and social. He cites Hemingway's remark that "all modern American literature comes from one book by Mark Twain called *Huckleberry Finn*" (*HF*, 305) and then goes on to compare Twain's work to *The Catcher in the Rye*. Cohen's comparison concludes in the following terms:

> In addition to being comic masterpieces and superb portrayals of perplexed, sensitive adolescence, these two novels thus deal obliquely and poetically with a major theme in American life, past and present—the right of the nonconformist to assert his nonconformity even to the point of being 'handled with a chain.' In them, 1884 and 1951 speak to us in the idiom and accent of two youthful travellers who have earned their passports to literary immortality (*HF*, 310).

American life also must be seen before it can be known. In 1958 I was an undergraduate student in class at Royce Hall at UCLA when Cohen lectured in his inimitable rabbinical style on the scene in which Huck decides he is willing to go to hell to save Jim. I came away from the lecture feeling my life had been changed and since that moment have been a student of Cohen's even now after he has left us. Many years later, I learned from an interview with Cohen in *New Literary History* (40, 4, 925) what was unknown to me at the time: I had the privilege to have been present at a lecture by the first Jew in the English Department of UCLA. Some of the passion in that inspiring address must have been personal and some of Cohen's infectious love of *Huckleberry Finn* was about how literature applied to life, both mine and his.

But I also feel that the final direction of Cohen's genre theory goes beyond the themes of American life, to life in general and that—as Cohen often asserted—the knowledge gained from literature is not different in kind from that of any other discipline. Thinking and learning begins with categories, kinds, or genres; these are the means by which we sort out the flux of life. Artistic interpretation teaches us that learning and knowledge require an understanding that these categories must remain flexible, capable of self-correction, from innovation to variation, even at times leading to the replacement or rejection of a category. The belief that genres are governed by laws or by any other concept of resistance to change is a form of dogmatism that leads to the stagnation of knowledge.

In conclusion, I wish to consider briefly my own sub-genre pursued in this volume and the two previous ones, theory explained by way of film and television programmes. This method was developed in the classroom. Struggling with the complex ideas and obscure language of theorists, my students referred to films that they believed exemplified some of the ideas we were discussing. As I began to use movies in the classroom, the students began to grasp these difficult concepts and, I came to realize, were far more at home with visual media than with printed texts. At this point the education was two-sided: while I explained literary theory to them, they tuned me in to movies and, later, television programmes.

This sub-genre resulted from listening as well as teaching. Genres are the basis of learning that in its most advanced form is a conversation between seekers of knowledge or between an art object and a responder. Listening and seeing is no less important than speaking and creating. Theoreticians would say genres are key to making art and to the interpretation of art, to expression and to response. Genres indicate to us the kind of message being transmitted and point toward the aim of the messenger. Our civilization rests upon understanding the new—from technological innovation to original ideas—and reconciling differences between people. To the attainment of these goals, the key is genre.

Bibliography

INTRODUCTION

—Mikhail Bakhtin, *The Dialogic Imagination: Four Essays*, trans. Caryl Emerson and Michael Holquist, Austin, University of Texas Press, 1981.

—Gilles Deleuze and Félix Guattari, *Anti-Oedipus*, London, Bloomsbury, 2013.

—Dorrit Cohn, "Does Socrates Speak for Plato? Reflections on an Open Question," *New Literary History*, 32, 2001, 3, 485-500.

—Jacques Derrida, "The Law of Genre", *Glyph*, 7, trans. Avital Ronell, 1980.

—Alastair Fowler, *Kinds of Literature: An Introduction to a Theory of Genres and Modes*, Oxford, Oxford University Press, 1982.

—Northrop Frye, *Anatomy of Criticism: Four Essays*, Princeton, Princeton University Press, 1957.

—Gérard Genette, *The Architext: An Introduction*, trans., Jane E. Lewin, Berkeley, University of California Press, 1992.

—Hans Robert Jauss, *Toward an Aesthetic of Reception*, trans., Timothy Bahti, Minnesota, University of Minnesota Press, 1982.

—Samuel Johnson, *Life of Milton*, London, Everyman, volume 1, 1968.

——A Review of Soame Jenyns' *Free Enquiry into the Nature and Origin of Evil*, London, 1757.

—John L, Rowlett, *Genre Theory and Historical Change: Theoretical Essays of Ralph Cohen*, Charlottesville, University of Virginia Press, 2017.

—Edward Tomarken, *Genre and Ethics: The Education of an Eighteenth-Century Critic*, Newark, Delaware: Associated University Press, 2002.

——*Filmspeak: How to Understand Literary Theory by Watching Movies*, New York, Bloomsbury, 2012.

——*Why Theory? Cultural Critique in Film and Television*, Manchester, Manchester University Press,, 2017.

—Mark Twain, *The Adventure of Huckleberry Finn*, with special aids by Ralph Cohen, New York, Bantam, 1965.

—Yuri Tynyanov, *Archaists and Innovators*, trans. Ann Shukman, Leningrad, 1929.

CHAPTER ONE

—Anis Bawarshi, "The Genre Function", *College English*, 62, 2, 2000, 335-360.
—Teresa de Lauretis, "Becoming Inorganic", *Critical Inquiry*, 29, 4, 2003, 547-70.

—Michel Maffesoli, "The Return of the Tragic in Postmodern Societies", *New Literary History*, 35, 2004, 1, 133-49.

—Igor Shaitanov, "Aleksandr Veselovskii's Historical Poetics: Genre in Historical Poetics", *New Literary History*, 32, 2, 2001.

CHAPTER TWO

—Emily Apter, "Taskography: Translation as a Genre of Literary Labor", *Publications of the Modern Language Association*, 122, 5, 2007.

—Elisabeth Bronfen, "Femme Fatale: Negotiations of Tragic Desire", *New Literary History*, 35, 1, 103-16.

—Dorothea von Mücke, "Profession/Confession", *New Literary History*, 34, 2, 257-74.

—William Morris, "Useful Work versus Useless Toil", in *William Morris: Selected Writings and Designs*, ed. Asa Briggs, London, Harmondsworth, 1980.

CHAPTER THREE

—Jonathan L. Crane, "Outsourced: Crime Stories, New World Horror, and Genre", *Popular Culture*, 33, 2 (2011), 117-36.

—Joseph Farrell, "Classical Genre in Theory and Practice", *New Literary History*, 34, 3, 2003, 383-408.

—Peter Hitchcock, "The Genre of Postcoloniality", *New Literary History*, 34, 2003, 2, 299-330.

CHAPTER FOUR

—Ann W. Astell and Susannah Brietz Monta, "Genre and the Joining of Literature and Religion: A Question of Kinds", *Religion & Literature*, 46, 2/3, 2014, 95-110.

—Dorrit Cohn, "Does Socrates Speak for Plato? Reflections on an Open Question", *New Literary History*, 32, 2001, 3, 485-500.

—Michael Trattner, "Derrida's Debt to Milton Friedman", *New Literary History*, 34, 2003, 4, 791-806.

CHAPTER FIVE

—Micah Mattix, "Periodization and Difference", *New Literary History*, 35, 2004, 4, 685-97.

—Thomas Pavel, "Literary Genres as Norms and Good Habits", *New Literary History*, 34, 2003, 2, 201-210.

—John L. Rowlett, "Ralph Cohen on Literary Periods: Afterword as Foreword", *New Literary History*, 50, 2019, 1, 129-39.

—Lois Parkinson Zamora, "Eccentric Periodization: Comparative: Perspectives on the Enlightenment and the Baroque", *PMLA*, 128, May 2013, 690-697.

CHAPTER SIX

—Thomas S. Eliot, *Old Possum's Book of Practical Cats*, London. Faber, 1939.

—Svend Erik Larson, "Landscape, Identity, and War", *New Literary History*, 35, 2004, 3, 469-490.

—James D. Lilley, "Henry Mackenzie's Ruined Feelings: Romance, Race, and the Afterlife of Sentimental Exchange", *New Literary History*, 38, 4, 2007, 649-664.

—Karl Marx, *Capital*, London, Classics of World Literature, 2013.

—Vlastimil Zuska, "Towards A Cognitive Model of Genre: Genre as a Vector Categorization of Film", *Theoria: An International Journal for Theory*, 15, 3, 2000, 481-495.

Other Theory Writings by the Author

Filmspeak: How to Understand Literary Theory by Watching Movies, Bloomsbury, 2012

This book analyses five major theoreticians from the 1960s and 70s when literary theory was first accepted as a separate discipline: Michel Foucault, Wolfgang Iser, Jacques Lacan, Fredric Jameson, and Hélène Cixous. The ideas of these seminal thinkers are illustrated by way of popular films for two purposes: 1) to show how the concepts have filtered into our culture 2) to translate the erudite, arcane language of theory into terminology comprehensible to the general reader.

Designed as an introduction for undergraduates to theory, the films are chosen by students in the author's classes, ranging from *The Dark Knight* to *Kill Bill* and from *The Social Network* to *The Devil Wears Prada*. By way of mainstream films, students realise that they do not have to wade through incomprehensible jargon to understand important ideas related to art criticism and to our daily life.

Why Theory? Cultural Critique in Film and Television, Manchester University Press, 2017

This book examines six theorists from the period 1970-2000: Clifford Geertz, Hayden White, Julia Kristeva, Homi K. Bhabha, Pierre Bourdieu, and Martha Nussbaum. The movies and television programmes are selected from the last two decades of the twentieth century, ranging from *The West Wing* (1999), and *Spiderman Two* (2004) to *Frozen* (2013) and *Twelve Years a Slave* (2013).

Ideal for students of literature and cultural studies, *Why Theory?* will also be useful for teachers and general readers looking for a new approach to a complex discipline that provides a new basis for its value.

Index

9 781838 185909